Usi

Lesson Observation

to Improve Learning

**FURTHER
EDUCATION**

YOU MIGHT ALSO LIKE

The A-Z Guide to Working in Further Education
978-1-909330-85-6
Jonathan Gravells and Susan Wallace

Becoming an Outstanding Personal Tutor: Supporting Learners through Personal Tutoring and Coaching
978-1-910391-05-1
Andrew Stork and Ben Walker

Embedding English and Maths: Practical Strategies for FE and Post-16 Tutors
978-1-910391-70-9
Terry Sharrock

Learning Technology: A Handbook for FE Teachers and Assessors
978-1-912096-93-0
Daniel Scott

Most of our titles are also available in a range of electronic formats. To order please go to our website www.criticalpublishing.com or contact our distributor, NBN International, 10 Thornbury Road, Plymouth PL6 7PP, telephone 01752 202301 or email orders@nbninternational.com.

Using
Lesson Observation
to Improve Learning

Practical Strategies for FE and Post-16 Tutors

TERRY SHARROCK

**FURTHER
EDUCATION**

First published in 2019 by Critical Publishing Ltd

British Library Cataloguing in Publication Data
A CIP record for this book is available from the British Library

ISBN: 978-1-912096-39-8

This book is also available in the following e-book formats:

MOBI ISBN: 978-1-912096-38-1
EPUB ISBN: 978-1-912096-37-4
Adobe e-book ISBN: 978-1-912096-36-7

Cover design by Out of House Limited
Text design by Out of House Limited
Project Management by Out of House Publishing Solutions
Printed and bound in Great Britain by 4edge, Essex

Critical Publishing
3 Connaught Road
St Albans
AL3 5RX

www.criticalpublishing.com

Paper from responsible sources

Contents

Meet the author

Terry Sharrock

A qualified teacher and former Ofsted inspector, Terry has worked in education for over 30 years, both in this country and the USA. He has taught in schools, colleges and adult and community learning for over 25 years.

Terry was a coach and cohort leader on the National Teaching and Learning Change Programme, designed to improve teaching, learning and assessment in a number of contexts.

He runs his own successful educational consultancy and regularly carries out observations of teaching and learning for a range of providers. Many of the ideas for this book have been developed from observations of outstanding teaching and learning sessions. He is the author of *Embedding English and Maths: Practical Strategies for FE and Post-16 Tutors*, also published by Critical Publishing.

Introduction

The idea for this book is a result of many years of carrying out lesson observations. As the years passed and the number of observations grew, it seemed to me that I found myself having the same conversations with teachers about recurring themes including differentiation, assessment, active learning, embedding English and maths, promoting equality and diversity, and British values. Some teachers view these aspects of teaching and learning as fads that come into and out of fashion (usually driven by the perceived requirements of Ofsted) and attempt to provide evidence of whichever is in fashion at the time. There is an amount of truth in this. There have been periods of time when certain aspects of teaching, learning and assessment have been more looked for than others. But I would argue that all the elements of teaching, learning and assessment that are discussed in this book are equally important and, when integrated naturally into the learner's experience, form the basis of quality teaching, learning and assessment. The purpose of this book is to help you understand the meaning and application of these aspects.

How to use this book

If you have been observed and some aspect of your teaching, learning and assessment has been highlighted as an area for improvement, you can use this book to understand more about that area and find ways to strengthen this aspect of your teaching.

Each chapter takes some commonly identified area for improvement and discusses:

» the meaning of the term;

» what it looks like when it is working well;

» some ideas of how you might strengthen this aspect of your teaching practice;

» actions to move forward in improving this area;

» some suggested reading to help you develop further.

You can work through the whole book, or you can look at a single chapter on a theme which you have identified (or has been identified for you), following an observation. Each chapter contains a suggested activity which you are encouraged to try out. A template is provided in Appendix 1 to help you record and reflect on your findings, possibly in consultation with other teachers.

The structure of each chapter

Following this Introduction, Chapter 1 looks at lesson observations in general and Chapters 2–9 contain the following features.

A bit of theory

This feature looks at research on the chapter subject and comments on how findings from this research can support you in your practice. While this will quote academic sources, the focus in this section is very much on the practical application of academic findings to your practice.

From the files

This feature takes case studies, which are real examples from practice that I have observed, and looks at one effective example and one less effective example. After reading the case studies you are invited to think about the examples and how they compare to your own experience, before reading about the key learning points of each one.

Think about it

This feature is an opportunity to reflect on your own practice. Use this section as a starting point for a conversation with others about how you might improve your teaching and learning. A template of a reflective journal is provided in Appendix 1. Use this to record what activities you tried, reflect on what happened and plan for future development.

Try this

This feature includes at least one suggested activity for you to try with your learners, connected to the subject of the chapter. The intention is that these activities are starting points for you to adapt and develop your own activities, best suited to your learners.

Summary (What should I do next?)

Each chapter contains a summary of the key points and suggestions as to what to do next to further develop in this area.

Further reading

This section suggests further reading that you might like to consider for further exploring the issues discussed in the chapter.

Chapter summaries

Chapter 1 Lesson observations

This chapter discusses the purpose of lesson observations in improving the quality of teaching, learning and assessment and includes an examination of the advantages and disadvantages of graded and ungraded observations. There will be advice for observers on how to judge the quality of learning and write reports that focus on learning, together with information on how to carry out post-observation discussions. There is advice on how to prepare for observations including how to deal with problems when being observed, such as discipline issues, inappropriate comments and IT malfunctions.

Chapter 2 Beginning and ending lessons

One of the frequently highlighted areas for improvement following observations is the beginning and ending of sessions. This chapter stresses the importance of beginnings and endings. It discusses what should be included in beginnings such as outlining the learning intentions and discusses ways to ensure that learners understand what is to be achieved in the lesson. It also discusses the use of starter activities and the importance of linking them to the main intentions of the lesson. It goes on to discuss the import- ance of a good ending to the session and allowing enough time to recap the learning. It looks at how to measure the effectiveness of the learning and different methods that might be used to engage learners in a productive summary of the learning.

Chapter 3 Differentiation

This chapter opens with a consideration of the use of the term 'differentiation' and how we might usefully define it in the context of education. The chapter includes discussion of why it is important and how it can contribute to more effective learning. There is an examination of relevant literature on the subject and on best practice in applying differ- entiation in learning. There are also examples of effective and less effective practice in the use of differentiation. The chapter includes practical activities for tutors to use and reflect on.

Chapter 4 Assessment for learning

This chapter looks at methods of assessing learning. It focuses on formative or ongoing assessment, as much of the work on summative assessment is covered in the dis- cussion of summaries in Chapter 2. It examines different strategies to assess forma- tive learning, beyond the use of direct questions. It discusses ways to ensure that all learners' understanding is checked and not just the individual learner who has answered the question. The chapter includes practical examples of formative assessment and a review of current literature and thinking on the most effective ways to assess learning.

Chapter 5 Giving feedback

This chapter looks at feedback on learners' work. It discusses best practice in providing written and verbal feedback. It examines how to ensure that the feedback you give is adopted by learners and leads to improvement. It discusses how to make the most effective use of written feedback and draws on experience of best practice in developing skills through feedback on written work. The focus is on the development of written

English and gives examples of the most effective practice to produce marking that leads to improvement. The chapter includes suggestions on effective use of written, verbal and peer-to-peer feedback.

Chapter 6 Effective questioning

This chapter looks at the use of questioning. There is a discussion of the purpose of questioning, a consideration of some of the most common errors and how teachers can be more effective in the use of different forms of questions. This chapter also includes a review of literature and theories of different forms of questioning that encourage evaluative and analytical skills. There is an opportunity for teachers to reflect on the types of questions they use and activities to promote effective questioning.

Chapter 7 Embedding English and maths

This chapter looks in detail at the key issues around successful embedding of English and maths and includes a list of ten things providers can do to improve English and maths results. It discusses how judgements on the quality of embedding of English and maths are made, and how best to engage reluctant learners and encourage them to attend English and maths lessons. The chapter considers some common questions that teachers ask, such as 'Does every lesson have to show embedding of English and maths?'

Chapter 8 Promoting equality and diversity

This chapter looks at the issue of promoting awareness of equality and diversity in learning sessions. Many teachers are uncertain what their role is in promoting awareness of equality and diversity, how best to plan for its inclusion, or how to deal with issues if they arise during the lesson. The chapter firstly looks at what is meant by the promotion of equality and diversity, what the role of the tutor is in promoting this learning and some examples of good and poor practice in this area. It includes discussion of unconscious bias and its effect on teaching and learning. This chapter seeks to clarify what is expected of teachers to effectively promote awareness of equality and diversity. Finally, the chapter provides case studies of good and poor practice, together with practical activities to promote awareness of equality and diversity.

Chapter 9 Promoting British values

This relatively new requirement of the Common Inspection Framework is still causing teachers some anxiety as they look to meet their requirement to promote British values. This chapter starts with a discussion of what is meant by British values and goes on to clarify the role of the teacher in promoting these values, together with examples of good and poor practice in this area. There is a consideration of how British values can be embedded into different vocational areas as well as tips on how to deal with controversial issues in discussions.

And finally...

I hope you find this book useful and that it can lead to viewing lesson observations as a useful tool to allow professionals to discuss and reflect on the business of providing the best educational experience for every learner. The most effective observer of your lesson should be yourself. If somebody else is in the room and commenting on the learning I hope that it is a chance to share ideas and discuss approaches that can have a positive effect on teaching, learning and assessment for your learners.

Chapter 1 Lesson observations

> *"Seek first to understand, then to be understood.*"
>
> **Stephen R Covey**

In his book, *The 7 Habits of Highly Effective People* (Covey, 1989), Stephen Covey gave the above advice about communication. I would argue it applies equally when observing teachers. First, question teachers to understand why they do what they do, before seeking to help them understand the judgements you make about their teaching.

Chapters 2 to 9 look in detail at different aspects of teaching and learning, including differentiation and the use of questioning, but this chapter looks at lesson observation and considers key factors around teaching and learning observations. It considers:

» what makes a good observation of the teaching and learning process;

» the purpose of observation;

» the advantages and disadvantages of graded and ungraded lessons;

» writing reports;

» post-observation discussion;

» how to prepare for observation.

What makes a good observation of the teaching and learning process?

If you could re-design your observation of the process, there are a number of factors that you would want to include. Ensure that you do the following.

» Involve staff in the design or planning of the system and ask them what they would like to achieve from lesson observations.

» Avoid long checklists of things that must be observed. Be aware that it is unlikely that one lesson will contain all elements of observation, such as embedding of English and maths, equality and diversity and promotion of British values. If there are no naturally occurring opportunities, find out how these are promoted throughout the course of study.

» Be flexible and judge each learning session on its own merit. Avoid strict rules on what is required for each grade. For example, an outstanding session might have no maths or British values embedded in the lesson.

» Talk to learners and ask them questions about what they are learning. Make your judgements based on how each learner is involved and enthused by the experience. Don't assume that if a learner doesn't speak that they are not learning.

» Avoid phrases like 'Personally I wouldn't have done it that way', 'What you should have done was…' and 'In my class I always…' It is not your job as an observer to say how you would have done it. Your job is to judge the amount of learning that has taken place. How do you know that your approach would work with these learners in this situation?

Think about how you can improve the experience for every individual and ensure that each student makes the most of their learning potential. Can you get to a position where staff are involved in designing the process and feel comfortable about having anyone come into lessons in an atmosphere of open exchange of ideas and experimentation?

The purpose of lesson observations

When I am called in to providers to carry out observations, one of the first questions I ask is: 'Why are you carrying out observations?' It's an apparently simple question but one that you need to know the answer to if you wish to achieve the purpose of the observation process. The reasons for carrying out lesson observation are:

» to monitor the quality of teaching and learning;

» to improve the quality of teaching and learning;

» to help with the development of staff.

Let's look at each of these in turn.

To monitor the quality of teaching and learning

This is useful for ensuring that all learners are receiving at least a reasonable experience of learning. It can also identify groups who are experiencing difficulties, perhaps caused by small numbers of learners disrupting the learning or where teachers are struggling to maintain a good learning atmosphere. This is about checking and maintaining a good standard of quality. Lesson observations, which might only be once a year, should not be the only way of monitoring this quality. Regular learning walks and open communication between staff should also be a key feature of the process.

To improve the quality of teaching and learning

This moves on from monitoring quality, to identifying areas where learning can improve. Lesson observations on their own will not be enough to ensure improvement but they can be an important part of the process. Used well, lesson observations can be opportunities for staff to try out new ideas and learn from each other. Unfortunately, current practice makes this very difficult when staff are afraid of judgements (whether they are graded or not), and too often see observation as a hoop to jump through, rather than an opportunity to discuss practice.

To help with the development of staff

If lesson observation is restricted to observing once a year, then a real opportunity to develop staff and improve teaching and learning has been missed. Increasingly, providers are finding ways for teachers to work together with frequent 'learning walks' or opportunities to sit in on each other's sessions and learn from each other. In this way, teachers can be more involved in the process and manage their own development.

Graded or ungraded observations?

It is very difficult to assess how much learning has taken place in any lesson, but that is what observers are asked to do. It seems unfair and arbitrary to make a decision on the amount of progress made by learners by sitting in the lesson and watching. Everybody involved from quality managers, senior managers, to observers and the observed have to recognise the flaws in the system and work together to decide how best the observation process can be used to fulfil its primary aim – to improve the learning experience for every individual.

Observation systems need to recognise the stress and pressurised nature of the observation process. Too often the observer is keen to tell the teacher the areas for improvement in the lesson. This promotes a 'parent–child' interaction where the observer is the expert telling the teacher how they could improve. This is reinforced by the need to assign a grade to reflect the quality of the learning experience. Given the uncertain nature of judging learning, this seems a process fraught with danger.

In 2015 Ofsted moved away from grading individual lessons. Inspectors will observe as many lessons as possible and award an overall grade for the quality of teaching and learning for the provider. In 2013, the University and College Union (UCU) commissioned a survey of 4,000 teachers and found that:

» 75 per cent of teachers surveyed disagreed that graded observations helped them to improve as classroom practitioners;

» 85 per cent felt that graded observations were not an effective way to assess staff competence and performance;

» 77 per cent felt that ungraded observations were more effective in assessing staff performance and competence.

(O'Leary, 2013)

This survey showed a clear preference for ungraded observations and this is what Ofsted have moved to. However, many providers still apply grading to lessons in order to monitor the quality of teaching and learning, and at least partly to present evidence to Ofsted. This presents a dilemma, with many teachers unhappy about the grade they receive. Feedback requires careful handling and an approach which values the contribution of the teacher and looks at grading as a starting point for improvement. Asking teachers to decide on the focus of the observation would be a good starting point. Observees could be given a choice of what aspect of the lesson they would like feedback on. For example, they could ask for feedback on their use of questions, or explanation and management of group activities. In this way teachers can have a sense of ownership and feel that lesson observation is something that is done with them rather than to them. Through a clearly understood set of criteria, teachers can see where learning could be improved and be involved in action planning methods of improvement.

Writing observation reports

When observers provide written feedback to staff, they are tasked with making judgements, sometimes hastily and based on limited evidence. In most cases it would be more useful, before making a judgement, to record what you see and note your view, before discussing it with the teacher after the lesson. For example, you might note:

> "In the opening activity one group was not engaged for 10 of the 15 minutes. Three members of the group were discussing something that happened last night."

This is a record of what you saw and can be followed up by noting questions for discussion afterwards such as, 'Why do you think Amir was not engaged in his group's discussion?' or 'I noticed that five of the fourteen students kept their coats on during the lesson. What is the college policy on this?' In this way, teachers have a chance to discuss the findings before any judgement is made. Reports should reflect the amount of and quality of learning that has taken place. They should clearly indicate what learners know by the end of the lesson and accurately record how each individual was involved, stretched and challenged during the learning experience.

Post-observation discussions

Post-observation discussion is one of the most important features of lesson observations but one that is often not given enough attention. Sometimes it is squeezed into the 15-minute break when the teacher should be having a well-earned rest. Sometimes there is not even that much time and discussion becomes the observer telling the teacher the strengths and areas for improvement, without much time for discussion.

Feedback, particularly where the observer has to award a grade, can be a difficult process. The effect of awarding a grade can be pivotal in deciding whether post-observation discussions are useful or confrontational. On a number of occasions, I have carried out post-observation discussions where the observee has engaged fully in the debate and we have talked enthusiastically about the learning. However, as soon as a grade is mentioned, if it is not the one that the observee was expecting, the conversation shuts down and the observee adopts a defensive stance and feels the need to justify their decisions in the lesson. The discussion becomes less productive and deteriorates into comment and counter-comment, which doesn't benefit anyone. The observation process should be a two-way activity and should always be productive in improving teaching and learning. In starting your verbal feedback, I recommend avoiding the standard 'How do you think it went?' question. In my opinion you only ask this question when you already know the answer. It also gives the teacher the opportunity to say 'I think it went really well', when the observer's viewpoint is very different! Focus the discussion on learners and learning within the session. A good opening question might be, 'Tell me about your learners?' This will start the conversation with a focus on the learners and shows the teacher that you are interested in the learning process and how well learners are developing skills. Make the focus of the questions less about the teacher's actions and more about the learners' reaction. This will keep the focus on the learning and off the teacher performance.

How to prepare for lesson observations

Ideally, teachers should be happy for observers to come into any lesson. If what you are doing every lesson is addressing individual needs and ensuring that all learners have the opportunity to learn, then this is what observers should see. However, this is rarely the case. Teachers will usually get some form of notice that observations are taking place, perhaps in a window of a one- or two-week period. In an observation period, teachers are more conscious of preparing for lesson observations. When you know that you are being observed, use the following checklist.

» Ensure there is a clear lesson plan with learning outcomes that are explained and shared with learners.

» All learning materials and presentations should be free of spelling and grammar errors. If you spot one during the lesson, use it as a learning experience and ask learners if they can spot the error in the material.

» If you encounter disciplinary issues or learners make inappropriate comments, don't panic. Stay calm. Acknowledge that you have noted the comment or behaviour and make a judgement whether you want to deal with it straight away or note it and deal with it later.

» If there is a malfunction with your IT, don't panic. Remember it is not the malfunction that is the issue but how you react to it. Ensure that any IT that doesn't work doesn't interfere with learning time. Decide how much time you want to spend trying to get the IT to work. Make sure it is no more than a few minutes. If it doesn't work, change the plan and do something else.

Summary (What should I do next?)

» Think about the purpose of lesson observations and make sure that whatever system you use is effective in meeting that purpose.

» Decide on graded or ungraded lesson observations. Whatever you decide, make sure it is a positive system that encourages teachers.

» In writing reports, focus on learning and the impact on learning. Whether as an observer or a teacher, judge the effectiveness of what you do on how well it contributes to the learning experience of every learner.

» In post-observation feedback, view the discussion as between two equals, rather than a teller and a listener. As an observer, show that you are interested in learners and learning rather than what the teacher is doing.

» Prepare for lesson observations but remember the best preparation is to make the good habit of teaching and learning part of your everyday teaching.

Further reading

O'Leary, M (2017) *Reclaiming Lesson Observations*. Abingdon: Routledge.

In this book, Professor Matt O'Leary of Birmingham University pulls together several articles on lesson observation and how to make the best use of observation to improve teaching and learning. It includes ideas for new approaches to lesson observations and advice on using observations to improve the quality of teaching and learning.

McVey, D (2016) Observation – Key Message: Guidance for Observers. [online] Available at: www.linkedin.com/pulse/observation-key-messages-guidance-observers-deborah-mcvey/ (accessed 4 September 2018).

This is a really useful article on writing observation reports. It provides good advice on how to write judgements and decide on how much evidence is sufficient to make a judgement. The article concludes with a useful ten-point checklist on writing reports.

McVey, D (2017) Post Observation Conversations with Teachers, about Learners: Guidance for Observers. [online] Available at: www.linkedin.com/pulse/post-observation-conversations-teachers-learners-guidance-mcvey/ (accessed 12 October 2018).

Another excellent article from Deborah McVey. This time the focus is on post-observation discussions. There is useful advice on asking open, genuine questions and focusing on recording what happened, using this as a basis for post-observation discussions, rather than giving judgements.

References

Covey, S R (1989) *The 7 Habits of Highly Effective People*. Salt Lake City, UT: FranklinCovey Co. [online] Available at: https://books.google.com/books/about/The_7_Habits_of_Highly_Effective_People.html?id=linHBwAAQBAJ (accessed 6 September 2018).

O'Leary, M (2013) (UCU) Developing a Framework for the Effective Use of Lesson Observation in Further Education. [online] Available at: www.ucu.org.uk/article/7105/Damning-report-calls-whole-process-of-lesson-observations-into-question (accessed 4 September 2018).

Chapter 2 Beginning and ending lessons

"No good ending can be expected in the absence of the right beginning."

The Book of I Ching

Introduction

It should go without saying that beginnings and endings are crucial parts of any lesson. Setting out what is to come and summarising what has happened are the foundations of making learning memorable and effective. So why do so many lessons start with learners wandering in and chatting while the teacher takes the register or sorts out some last-minute resources? And why do so many lessons end with a hurried recap of what was done and the teacher giving instructions for the next lesson with learners putting their coats on or walking out of the door? Think about the beginnings and endings of your lessons and assess how effective you think they are.

In planning your lesson, how much do you think about how you are going to share the learning intentions (what you would like learners to learn in this lesson)? Ask yourself, am I simply reading these out or am I involving learners in understanding what it is we are going to explore together? If you read out the learning intentions, how are you ensuring that learners understand them and even have some opportunity to agree that that is what they want to learn today? Often learners are told the learning intentions. They are displayed, read out and followed up by asking, 'Any questions?' In many years of observing over hundreds of lessons I think I could count on the fingers of two hands how many times learners have actually asked any questions about the learning intentions of the lesson. See the activity below for ways to test understanding of the learning intentions.

There are, in my experience, few occasions where teachers check learners' understanding of learning intentions. It is as if simply telling learners what the objectives are is enough, and sometimes this seems to be done for the benefit of an observer rather than a genuine interest in invoking learning and getting learners involved in what will be explored in the session.

Before planning any lesson, ask yourself how you will test your learners' understanding of the learning intentions. For example, if you say that one of the learning intentions for a catering lesson is to 'describe the causes and effects of food contamination and food poisoning', how could you then test that learners understand what this is and what they should be able to do by the end of the session? How will you know if this intention has been achieved?

This chapter looks at why it is important to get any lesson off to a good start and to have a memorable and effective summary of learning. It explores a couple of examples that demonstrate effective and not so effective ways to start and end lessons, and finally looks at some practical ideas for you to try to vary the way you start and end lessons.

Starting your lesson

Consider the following four aspects of the start of a lesson.

1. Explaining the learning intentions

Vary the way in which you explain the learning intentions. You don't always have to do this at the start of the lesson. Experiment with how and when you explain the intentions. Try giving learners just the title of the session and asking them to create the learning intentions. Sometimes the explanation of the learning intentions seems to be done more for the benefit of an observer than the learners. Don't fall into this trap.

2. Keep it manageable

How many learning intentions might be expected in each session? Quite often we try to be too ambitious in the coverage of what we can achieve in one session. Think about whether it is better to master a few learning intentions, rather than list a number which might overwhelm or confuse learners.

3. Recap previous learning

Think of ways to recap the learning from previous sessions in order to show learners how what is to be learnt today is linked to past and future learning, and how it fits into the overall scheme of work.

4. Use a starter activity

It's usually a good idea to have something for learners to do as soon as they enter your classroom. It sets the tone and gets learners in the right frame of mind for the lesson. The debate is, does this activity have to be linked to the main topic of the session? I would argue that it does, but with a little imagination and planning this doesn't have to be difficult. Look for ways to use the learning in the lesson to reinforce the starter activity. For example, if your starter is a puzzle where learners have to follow instructions carefully, find activities in the main learning where the importance and accuracy of following instructions can be reinforced.

A bit of theory

Effect sizes

There is surprisingly little research done on the effectiveness of beginnings and endings of lessons. In his book, *Evidence-Based Teaching* (Petty, 2006), Geoff Petty discusses the work of John Hattie on 'effect sizes' (Hattie, 2009). Put simply, this tries to put a numerical value on the varying effectiveness of teaching and learning strategies. For example, a strategy which has an effect size of 1.0 might equate to:

» improving learning by 50 per cent or improving learners' achievement by one year;

» a two-grade improvement in GCSE, say from an E to a C or a 2 to a 4.

Hattie describes an effect size of 0.4 as the point where a teaching and learning strategy might be described as effective. Petty goes on to describe how using a combination of opening strategies can have an outstanding 'effect size' of 2.66. These strategies include one or more of the following:

» a visual representation of the learning intentions of the lesson;

» setting learning intentions in terms of what will be learnt rather than what will be done;

» good use of questioning to review and consolidate previous learning.

Look back at the results of an effect size of 1.0 above to realise how much of an improvement this would be.

There is a general anecdotal consensus that the beginnings and endings of lessons can have a significant impact on the amount and quality of learning.

Look at the following two examples which highlight effective and less effective beginnings and endings of lessons.

From the files

The two case studies that follow are examples of good practice (case study 2) and less effective practice (case study 1). Although these were real lessons that I have observed, they contain many common themes of effective and less effective practice. For example, in case study 1 learners waiting while the tutor takes the register is, regrettably, a common occurrence at the start of lessons. Similarly, the rushed ending and hurried summary of learning on show in case study 1 is also a common theme.

Case study 1

This was a class in a general further education (FE) college. There were ten learners present. The learning intentions were written on the board and included: 'to understand the properties of two-dimensional (2D) and three-dimensional shapes (3D)'. The tutor read these out to learners, but there was no discussion of what they meant or questioning of learners as to whether they understood what the terms meant. All the learners were on vocational courses ranging from construction to hairdressing but there was no exploration of how this knowledge might be of use to them in their vocational areas, or in any aspect of their lives.

The tutor took the class register. Learners waited (with varying degrees of impatience) for their turn to answer their names. At the same time, displayed on the whiteboard behind the tutor was an illustration of an optical illusion. It was an example of street art and gave a very clever effect of a huge hole in the road with someone staring into it. The illusion was that it was a two-dimensional drawing in the road, which had been made to look three dimensional. Some learners had noticed it, but the tutor had not referred to it, asked learners to look at it, or involved them in any activity or thinking related to the illustration. When the register was taken, the tutor asked learners to look at the illustration and described it as an example of an optical illusion. Why hadn't he asked them to look at it and work out what it was while he was taking the register? The tutor went on to describe a visit that he had taken to an optical illusion museum dedicated to the work of the Dutch artist Maurits Escher. Although he told the story, he did not make any connection between the illustration and the learning intentions, although it seemed clear that there was an opportunity to discuss the concept of 2D and 3D shapes. From this point the class went on to practising exercises on worksheets to identify 2D and 3D shapes. This seemed to me to be a real missed opportunity to make a purposeful and engaging opening to the lesson, all the more surprising since the tutor had obviously gone to the trouble of finding some engaging resources that, if used more effectively, would have a good chance of engaging learners from the start.

At the end of the session the tutor used a piece of software which involved learners using their mobile phones to complete a quiz on what had been learnt in the session. The quiz involved a number of questions asking learners to identify properties of 2D and 3D shapes and in some cases give the formula for working out the area of different shapes. Learners were engaged in this and liked the idea of submitting answers to questions which were then displayed on the board. They participated enthusiastically and were keen to see who 'got the right answers'. The problem was that this activity, while engaging and energising, only proved the point that most of the learners had not achieved the learning intentions. The results showed that about 70 per cent of the class were not able to identify 2D and 3D properties and even fewer were able to confidently work out the areas or volume of even simple shapes.

Key learning points

» Give learners something to do while taking the register. Make sure this is connected to the learning intentions of the lesson.

» Always explain to learners how what they will learn today can be of use to them in their intended work, further study or in their lives generally.

» If you use technology to enhance the learning experience, make sure it does just that. No matter how enthusiastically learners engage in this kind of activity, the purpose is to find out if learners have made progress in their understanding.

Case study 2

This was a functional skills maths class for catering students with five learners present. The lesson opened with a good recap of previous learning on fractions and percentages, through the use of questioning and a matching activity carried out in pairs where learners matched card definitions to terms that were covered in the previous session. Most learners could confidently name the terms and often referred back to what they had done in the previous session to help them recall the definitions.

The lesson started with a clear explanation of the topic, which was ratios, and there was good use of examples from the vocational area of catering to relate the topic of ratios to their use in catering – for example, scaling up or scaling down recipes and the ratio of waiting staff to guests in a catering function. The learning was related to learners' vocational area of catering and they were asked to give personal examples of ratios. One that sticks in my mind was the learner who was very keen to share the ratio of ingredients in her national dish (Burek).

With about 15 minutes of the lesson remaining, the tutor announced that it was time to summarise the learning. Learners were asked to work in pairs to play dominoes matching up equivalent ratios in order to test their understanding of the learning intentions. While they were engaged in the activity, the tutor moved around the group questioning and testing understanding of the topic. He had a system of scoring each learner's understanding of the topic from 1–5, where 1 was a thorough understanding and 5 was insufficient understanding. He used his scoring system to allocate a score to each learner after each lesson and in this way built up, over time, a way to monitor the progress of each learner. He asked learners to write on a sticky note one thing they had learnt and one thing they would like to know more about. These notes were collected at the end of the lesson and used to inform the planning for the next session. Before leaving, learners were invited to suggest one new thing they had learnt today. Finally, the tutor closed by previewing what would be covered in the next lesson before thanking learners and inviting them to leave.

Key learning points

» There was a comprehensive summary of learning from the last session.

» Previous learning was linked to new learning in the current session.

» Learning intentions were clearly explained and related to their use in the vocational area.

» Learners were involved in giving examples of how today's learning related to their own experience.

» The summary of learning was thorough and allocated enough time to explore fully what had been learnt.

» The tutor employed a number of different tactics to assess how well learners understood the learning intentions of the session and this information was used to inform future learning.

» Learners were told what was coming next and how it fitted into the overall scheme of work.

Try this

Activity

Next time, after you have explained a task or shared the learning intentions and you ask, 'Any questions?' note if anyone asks a question. If they don't, try testing their understanding by choosing a learner and asking, 'OK (*name*) can you explain for the group what we are doing (or the meaning of the first learning intention)?' See what happens.

Here are a few ideas to enhance the opportunities for learning at the start and end of your lessons.

Add 'because' to the end of learning intentions

Consider asking learners to add 'because' to the end of learning intentions to get them to think about why the skills they are learning are important. For example, a learning intention that says 'learn techniques to write persuasively' could become 'learn techniques to write persuasively because it's important to know how to express yourself, for example in writing an email of complaint to get some compensation for faulty goods or service'. The process of adding 'because' to learning intentions will focus learners (and yourself) on why we need to learn what we are learning in the lesson.

Defining words

Give groups of learners a key word each from the learning intentions and ask them to come up with as many connecting words as possible in one minute. For example, a learning intention in construction might include the following: 'identify *all the* ingredients *in order to* analyse *and* understand *the* ratio *in the mixture of concrete*'.

Highlight key words

You could highlight key words within the learning intention (the words in italics above are some suggestions of the key words in this learning intention) or, better still, start the discussion by asking learners to highlight the key words. Once these are identified, ask learners to find a definition for them. This could be done as a whole-class activity with each group asked to choose a different word to define and explain to the rest of the group. Groups of learners could be invited to explain the definition of the key terms and give examples of how it might be used in another sentence. In this way, you will be able to judge more accurately how well learners have understood what the learning intention is, as well as exploring some quite difficult concepts such as the difference between 'identify', 'analyse' and 'understand'.

Create a puzzle

A variation on this theme is to reverse the procedure and display the learning intentions with definitions replacing key words. For example, look at the learning intention below. Explain to learners that their job is to replace the numbers 1, 2, 3 and 4 with a key word from the learning intention. To help them, the definition of the word is given. Each star represents a missing letter.

In a beauty therapy session, you might display the following:

1 how to *2* the *3* and *4*

1 = know the meaning of (*************)

2 = colour something slightly (********)

3 = the strip of hair growing on the ridge above a person's eye socket (************)

4 = short curved hairs growing on the edges of the eyelids serving to protect the eyes from dust (************)

Can you work it out? The answer is 'Understand how to tint the eyebrows and eyelashes'.

Visual representation

Instead of simply displaying the learning intentions on the board and reading them out, what about a visual representation of the learning objectives, perhaps summarising the key points in the form of a cartoon or series of drawings or photographs, and ask learners what they think they will learn today.

Missing words

Another way to introduce the learning intentions rather than simply displaying them and reading them out is to display them with letters missing and ask learners individually or in pairs to fill in the blanks. For example, can you work out these three learning intentions for a computer games design class?

1. Kn*w /wh*t /*nim*ti*n /m**ns

2. Und*rst*nd /th*t/th*r*/ *r* /diff*r*nt/ m*th*ds/, which/ c*n/ b*/ us*d /t* /cr**t* /*nim*ti*ns

3. B*/ *bl* /t*/ writ*/ a /pl*n/ th*t/ y*u /c*n /f*ll*w/ t*/ cr**t*/ a/ sh*rt / *nim*ti*n/ s*qu*nc*/

Answers

1. Know what animation means.
2. Understand that there are different methods which can be used to create animations.
3. Be able to write a plan that you can follow to create a short animation sequence.

You can vary this by dividing the group into teams and asking learners to guess the missing letters. Display the intentions with an * symbol to replace all the missing letters and fill in the blanks to add a sense of anticipation as learners wait to see if they have guessed correctly!

'Find the words' starter activity

Have a word displayed on the whiteboard as learners enter and ask them to make as many words as they can from the letters of the word shown. Preferably use a word connected with the topic for the lesson and one that will provide plenty of opportunities to create new words. For example, in an early years setting (and others) you might use the word 'confidentiality'. Invite learners to see how many new words they can make from that word. Allow words of three letters or more but no proper nouns. (There is an opportunity here to reinforce what a proper noun is.) Give them a point for every word and three points if they can explain how the word has some connection with their vocational setting. Setting a time limit of three or four minutes can also add a change of pace and ensure the activity doesn't go on for too long. You can set targets such as: 5 words 'Average'; 6–10 words 'Good'; and more than 10 words 'Expert'. Sharing your own target with learners can provide extra impetus. You might decide to set a not too challenging figure for yourself (say six words) to boost learners' confidence. After all, everyone wants to do better than the teacher!

In the example above, how many words can you make from the word 'confidentiality'? 'Confident', 'cot', 'diet', 'infant', 'antidote'. Any more? It's quite astonishing how many words can be made from it (see Appendix 2 for a list of 300 words that can be made).

There are some good opportunities to extend learning from this type of starter activity, including:

» extending vocabulary ('what does a "dietician" do?'); ('what exactly is a "tannoy"?');

» building on spellings from root words ('infant', 'infantile' and 'infanticide');

» identifying homophones such as 'die' and 'dye', 'tale' and 'tail', 'idol' and 'idle';

» discussing issues of equality and diversity ('is it ever acceptable to use the term "idiot?"');

» defining and discussing ethical issues such as 'cloning'.

And yes. All the words given as examples can be made from the letters of the word 'confidentiality'.

Use this kind of starter activity and make sure you link it to the main learning intentions of the lesson. For example, it should be easy to reference the words learners have found when discussing the whole issue of confidentiality in an early years setting. The warm-up activity has the added advantage of preparing learners for a period of learning. Just as you might warm up before some physical activity, explain to learners that this is a mental warm-up to move from outside-the-class thinking to inside-the-class thinking.

Ideas for endings

One of the main aims of reviewing the learning is to move the learning that has taken place from short-term memory (what we are thinking about and retaining now) to long-term memory (the state where we can recall information, understand and apply it to new learning). It's not just a matter of learning it so that we can recall it 'parrot fashion'. It's important that learners have the opportunity to reframe what they have learnt into terms that they can understand and which make sense to them. Too often as teachers, we strive to help learners understand concepts in *our* terms. Really effective learning happens when learners have opportunities to engage with ideas that help them reframe what they are learning in *their own* terms. Your definition of rendering in construction, say, might be easy for you to understand and relate to, but this does not mean it will be the same for your learners. How can you encourage learners to find their own meaning? This is when they start to engage in the kind of deep learning that enables them to take ownership of their learning. This is a crucial stage in the learning process if learners are going to be able to confidently learn, understand and apply concepts. So how can we encourage learners to revisit and review their learning in a way that encourages them to explore, review and rephrase it in terms that make sense to them? Here are a few ideas, but first of all make sure you leave enough time to carry out a meaningful review of the learning. You should leave at least 15 minutes at the end of the session to reinforce the learning. This is a vital part of the learning process and should not be glossed over quickly. Ending lessons effectively with meaningful summaries of learning is a key way to develop these skills. What follow are some ways in which you might approach the endings of lessons. The list is not exhaustive and should serve as a starting point for you to explore different ways to end lessons and measure how successful you have been in meeting the learning intentions.

Taking notes

Encouraging learners to take notes about what they've learnt and introducing ideas such as mind mapping (whether this is on paper or using mind-mapping software) is crucial to helping learners take ownership and responsibility for their own learning. Think for a moment about the process of note-taking and ask yourself how much time you spend teaching learners how to make effective notes. Have you ever discussed with learners the process of making effective notes? Reviewing and summarising information are high-level skills that need to be taught. The aim is to help learners reach a point where they can use new knowledge and skills confidently to apply them to different situations and solve new problems. In order to do this effectively, learners have to make sense of new skills in their own way, and making notes is the first step in this process.

Learner-set questions

Try a quiz where the learners set questions for each other on the key learning points of the lesson. Show them the learning intentions, divide the group into two or more groups and ask them to come up with questions for the other team. Ensure that the team setting the questions are confident that they know the answers.

Using questions to review learning

Use questions to help learners reflect on their learning. Below is a list of questions you might find useful. I'm not suggesting you use all of these, but you might like to pick a few and vary them for different lessons. Over a period, see which questions produce the most useful reflections.

» What new thing did I learn today?

» What was the most useful thing I learnt today?

» How will I use what I learnt today?

» What do I remember most from today's lesson?

» What do I feel most confident about?

» What do I need more help with?

» When will I start to use what I learnt in this lesson?

» Where can I get more information from?

» What progress did I make today?

» What do I need to do before the next lesson?

» How will I remember what I learnt today?

» What do I think we will learn in the next lesson?

Hot seating

Have key words from the lesson displayed on a board or whiteboard. Ask one student (a volunteer preferably) to come to the front and sit with their back to the key words. The student in the hot seat can call on three of their classmates to give them clues to the word without actually mentioning it. For example, if the word is 'parasite' you might give clues like 'feeds off another animal', 'can spread disease' and 'takes nourishment from other animals'.

Guess the word

Another variation of the hot-seating game is to have learners work in pairs or small groups to pick a card with a key term on it and try to explain it without referring to the word itself, along the lines of a game of charades.

'Yes or no' questions

This is a paired activity based on the 'Who Am I?' game. Working in pairs, have learners write down key words or phrases from the lesson on sticky notes. Ask learners to stick a word on their partner's forehead. The object of the game is to guess the word on your forehead by asking questions to which your partner replies 'yes' or 'no'. When one of the pair receives the answer 'no', the turn switches to the other person and so on until both learners guess the term.

Summary (What should I do next?)

Remember

» Beginnings and endings are crucial to effective learning.

» Beginnings set the tone for the lesson and recap and reinforce previous learning.

» Take time to ensure that learners understand and buy into learning intentions.

» Vary the way you present the learning intentions.

» If you use a starter activity, make sure you link it to the main lesson content and refer to it throughout the lesson and in the summary.

» Vary the methods you use to summarise and measure the amount and quality of learning that has taken place.

» Endings summarise current learning and link it to the next steps.

Further reading

Sztabnik, B (2015) The 8 Minutes that Matter Most. [online] Available at: www.edutopia. org/blog/8-minutes-that-matter-most-brian-sztabnik (accessed 12 October 2018).

This article by American English teacher Brian Sztabnik contains some useful thoughts about beginnings and endings, and has some practical suggestions to try. I like the idea of starting with good news or celebrating the achievement of learners to give the lesson a positive feel-good factor from the outset. A useful addition to a list of reflective activities at the end of a lesson is the idea of asking learners to write one thing they learnt from another learner during the lesson.

Didau, D (2012) *The Perfect Ofsted English Lesson*. Carmarthen, Wales: Independent Thinking Press.

This very useful book discusses the start and end of the 'perfect' lesson. Although primarily aimed at schools, there are many ideas, such as the ones included in Chapter 2 'The Start of the Lesson') and Chapter 4 ('The End of the Lesson'), which can easily be adapted to post-16 education. Page 30 gives a clear explanation of John Hattie's research on 'effect sizes' and their impact on learners' progress.

Online

Hendrick, C (2017) Teachers: Your Guide to Learning Strategies that Really Work. [online] Available at: www.theguardian.com/teacher-network/2017/oct/27/teachers-your-guide-to-learning-strategies-that-really-work (accessed 12 October 2018).

This useful short article from *The Guardian* Teacher Network brings together some research on effective strategies, including the importance of revisiting previous learning at the start of a lesson.

Whitelock, G (2017) Breaking the Ice. [online] Available at: https://sharingtla.wordpress. com/2016/09/11/breaking-the-ice/ (accessed 12 October 2018).

This is a brief article sharing the idea of starting or reviewing lessons with questions written on footballs that are passed around. You have to answer the question under your thumb when you catch the ball.

References

Ditkoff, M (2018) 20 Awesome Quotes on Beginnings. [online] Available at: www.innovationexcellence.com/blog/2011/01/24/20-awesome-quotes-on-beginning/ (accessed 12 October 2018).

Hattie, J (2009) *Visible Learning: A Synthesis of Over 800 Meta Analyses Relating to Achievement.* Abingdon: Routledge.

Petty, G (2006) *Evidence-Based Teaching: A Practical Approach* (2nd ed). Cheltenham: Nelson Thornes.

Chapter 3 Differentiation

> "*Differentiation is simply a teacher attending to the learning needs of a particular student... rather than teaching a class as though all individuals in it were basically alike.*"
>
> **Carol Anne Tomlinson**

Introduction

This chapter looks at the topic of differentiation and some of the most common areas for improvement identified in Ofsted reports. There is a discussion of definitions of the term, an examination of a variety of methods of differentiation and two case studies. The chapter goes on to examine the most common teaching and learning methods and assess how effective they are in promoting differentiated learning. Finally, it suggests two activities to promote better differentiation.

The comments below are a summary of some of the most common areas for improvement identified by Ofsted in a number of inspections.

> "*Learners with differing abilities all work on the same tasks at the same level.*"

> "*Teachers do not provide learning which takes into account the wide range of needs and abilities of their learners, particularly the most able.*"

> "*In too many lessons, teachers ask whole-group questions to which the same students respond.*"

While they are not direct quotes, they do highlight the kind of comments that indicate a need to improve teaching and learning through an improved use of differentiation. The first two points paint a picture of a lesson where all learners carry out the same activities regardless of ability; where the most able find it too easy and get bored and the least able find it too difficult and lose interest. The third point describes a lesson where only a few learners answer questions.

What is differentiation?

There are a number of definitions of the term 'differentiation' in an educational context (see 'A bit of theory' later in the chapter). Before we examine these, let's think about what we are trying to achieve when we differentiate. The aim of successful differentiation must be to treat each learner as an individual and build on their learning using their individual starting points.

Differentiation is about knowing your learners, knowing their strengths and weaknesses; knowing how they like to learn; knowing what motivates them and what puts them off; knowing which areas they are confident in and which areas give them difficulty. It is also about knowing something of their history. What have been their past experiences in education? Where have they had success and where have they come up against barriers and experienced failure? Learners come to you with a history and a wealth of experiences, not all of them necessarily positive. This is what you are working with (and sometimes against).

What is so good about differentiation and why should you do it?

Differentiation is a key element of successful learning. As far as possible, treating each learner as an individual is the ideal. Knowing what learners can do and where they need to improve is a vital element of outstanding teaching, learning and assessment. Learners who feel they are being treated as individuals (starting with something as simple as knowing and using their names) are generally much more successful and willing to engage with learning, particularly if they can see the progress they are making and the skills they are developing. Real individual learning plans that treat people as individuals and chart individual progress are powerful motivational tools that are currently underused.

Advice from Ofsted is interesting on this subject:

"Inspectors don't expect work and tasks in all lessons to be tailored to meet each student's individual abilities. This is an unrealistic expectation. However, teachers should make sure that all students have opportunities to fulfil their potential, regardless of their starting points or abilities. Inspectors will expect to see evidence of this through the course as a whole."

(Ofsted, 2018)

This suggests that Ofsted realises that it is nearly impossible to tailor learning to each individual, particularly in large classes, and that learning should be aimed at levels of learners. I would agree that this is the case in large classes, but where groups of learners number around 12 or fewer, I would suggest individual learning becomes much more achievable.

A bit of theory

Defining differentiation

The Training and Development Agency for Schools (TDA) describes differentiation as:

> "The process by which differences between learners are accommodated so that all students in a group have the best possible chance of learning."
>
> **(cited in Sistemaengland, 2005)**

David Didau, who writes very well on teaching English in schools, describes differentiation as:

> "The process of acknowledging that every (learner) is different and treating them accordingly."
>
> **(Didau, 2011)**

Geoff Petty defines differentiation as:

> "An approach to teaching that attempts to ensure all students learn well, despite their many differences."
>
> **(Petty, 2017)**

Types of differentiation

Educationalists identify a number of types of differentiation, including differentiation using feedback, by questioning, by support and by learning outcome. Let's look at each in turn and suggest how you might apply them to your own practice.

Differentiation using feedback

You work with learners all the time and are constantly giving them feedback, both verbal and written. In learning sessions, learners answer questions, interact with you and each other and carry out activities. You give them feedback on the quality of their answers and the standard of their work and hopefully try to extend their thinking and understanding. You are doing this to each individual learner all the time and through this you are differentiating by adapting your input to each learner's needs. Working with learners in class or individually – say, in a workplace – written and verbal feedback can be tailored to the needs of each individual and can prove to be a very effective method of differentiating. You may well do this without fully realising that you are differentiating between learners. You can talk to learners about what they know and assess how well they understand a topic and what they might need to do next to further or deepen their understanding.

Differentiation by questioning

You can make use of questioning to differentiate between learners at different levels. You might well be doing this unconsciously without realising it. When posing questions to the whole group, you might vary the level of questioning from simple recall ('What is the meaning of the term depreciation?') to analysis ('In what ways can a company most effectively allow for depreciation in their budgeting?'). In dealing with individual learners you can adjust your questioning to match the current level of understanding demonstrated by the learner and aim to stretch each individual to increase their confidence and understanding of the learning outcomes.

Differentiation by support

This is where learners work on the same activities and have the same learning outcomes but receive different levels of support from you or from learning assistants. This support can be in the form of individual coaching or the provision of different levels of support material. A good starting point is a class profile. As well as the results of initial assessments, such as levels and ability in English and maths, a really good class profile should serve as a reminder and prompt about each individual, including:

» attitudes to learning;

» details of how well they work as a member of a group;

» whether they are keen to participate in discussions and activities or whether they prefer to take a more passive role.

This information is crucial in deciding on the type and level of support provided to each individual.

Differentiation by learning outcome

Differentiation by outcome is setting learners the same task and expecting different outcomes from different levels of ability. This is usually seen in the form of stated learning outcomes that include phrases such as:

» all learners will be able to… (all learners will achieve a minimum standard of learning in the session);

» most learners will be able to… (the majority of learners are expected to reach a standard);

» some learners will be able to… (the more able learners will be able to achieve a higher level of learning).

This method suggests that there will be different levels of learning taking place and learners will access the level that best meets their needs. If done well, this has its place but it does run the risk of setting self-fulfilling prophecies of the standards of work that will be produced. Increasingly, educators are talking about mastery as an alternative to the use of differentiation.

Mastery versus differentiation

Differentiation by learning outcome may be well intentioned, with the view being that all learners can participate in a task but that there will be different expectations of the end result. However, recently it has come under fire from those who feel that it is limiting what learners can do. In other words, if you are asked to produce a minimum standard, that is what you will do.

Some educators are instead talking about 'mastery' of a subject, which suggests that all learners regardless of their ability can *'learn anything if that learning is presented in the right way'* (Blatchford, 2015).

This is quite an interesting and challenging concept but one that has taken hold, mainly fuelled by its successful use in high-performing educational systems in countries such as Japan, South Korea, China and Singapore. The key issue is that all learners are expected to 'master' the concepts of, for example, trigonometry in maths. The differentiation comes not in the topics or content taught but in the amount of support and intervention given to pupils who are finding the concepts difficult. Learners might be helped to 'mastery' of a topic through structured tasks and carefully thought-out questioning. This support and intervention has to be relevant and immediate for it to be effective. Another key feature is the fact that the whole group will not move on until all learners have mastered the concept. It is an interesting idea, in view of the increasing number of Ofsted reports containing comments such as 'too few teachers check and assess whether all students have fully understood a concept before moving on to another task'.

From the files

The following two case studies are from lessons observed in a general FE college. They demonstrate, in my opinion, examples of effective practice (case study 2) and not so effective practice (case study 1). After reading through them, consider the questions on case study 1, before looking at the commentary in Appendix 3, which contains some suggested answers. Case study 2 is an example of more effective practice and comments are included within the case study. Neither of the examples are perfect, because they are from real life, but case study 1 illustrates the most common areas for improvement that I observe in implementing effective differentiation.

Case study 1

This was an English lesson on writing a letter of complaint, with a small group of 16 to 18 year-olds. The learning outcomes were:

» for all learners to know the difference between a formal and informal letter;

» all learners will be able to plan and write a letter of complaint.

The tutor file had some information about each learner. An example is shown below:

Name	Target grade	Maths GCSE	English GCSE	Functional skills English initial assessment	Functional skills maths initial assessment
MS	Pass	E	D	Level 1	Entry 3

The tutor started the session with a brief presentation of the difference between formal and informal language.

All learners were given a piece of writing from a holiday company, responding to a poor review of their service. Learners were then given questions to assess their understanding of the content. Some learners finished early and were waiting for others to finish. Some waited patiently and others chatted or checked their mobile phones.

The tutor led a class discussion about writing a letter of complaint. Some learners made contributions, mainly to answer the questions asked by the tutor. Most learners did not contribute to the discussion. Students were given some time to discuss in pairs what should be included in the letter of complaint before being invited out to the front to talk individually about the information they would include in this letter. Students spoke with varying degrees of confidence and ability. All students were thanked and the group was encouraged to give each person a round of applause.

Towards the end of the lesson, students completed a self-assessment sheet, marking green, amber or red to a number of questions designed to assess their level of understanding of the topic (green indicating that they were confident they could write a letter of complaint independently; amber that they were mostly confident; and red indicating that they were not sure how to do it). All students carried out the self-assessment. The tutor concluded by asking learners if they had completed the assessment before dismissing them.

Questions

1. What comments would you make about the stated learning outcomes?

2. What use could be made of the information provided in the session file? What other information would be useful to have on each learner?

3. Could the task of composing a complaint be related to the different vocational areas?

4. How effective is the learning in the activity of bringing learners to the front to discuss the information they would include in the complaint?

5. What comments would you make about the final assessment activity?

Case study 2

This was a discrete functional skills speaking and listening class for 16 to 19 year-old beauty therapy students. Of the 17 learners, 16 were present at the start of the session. Information on each learner was kept in a class profile, an example of which follows.

Example of a class profile entry			
Name	Profile	Independent learner?	Progress (include date)
MS	Lots of support required. Very easily distracted by those around her. M*** needs regular breaks. Lacks confidence in her own ability.	No.	Concentrated well in lesson on persuasive writing and showed good understanding. Worked well with JB (13/11).

As you can see, the information on the learner goes beyond the outcome of initial and diagnostic assessment and previous grades, although these are recorded elsewhere. This kind of individualised profile, if used properly, provides a real chance of implementing highly effective differentiation of learning.

Learners were researching a recent news story on the sacking of a well-known TV celebrity. The learning outcomes were to:

» develop and practise research skills;

» find information to support your viewpoint;

» develop and practise skills in presenting to an audience;

» develop and practise making contributions to discussions.

Each learner was given a sheet of paper with the learning objectives and the following success criteria:

» Demonstrate effective research skills.

» Demonstrate presentation skills in a formal setting.

» Listen and respond appropriately to spoken language, including to questions and feedback to presentations.

» Use spoken Standard English effectively in speeches and presentations.

The learning objectives and success criteria sheet included a space for personal reflections. Learners used this sheet to reflect on what they had done throughout the lesson as well as at the end. Learners spoke of how they appreciated the chance to write in the personal reflections section to review their learning as they went along.

Learners worked in pairs, with one half of the group tasked to find information to support the sacking and the other half charged with finding facts to support the argument that the sacking was unjustified.

The tutor had used the individual group profile to ensure that learners were paired in the most effective way to benefit each learner. This tutor had been with the group for some time and knew which learners worked well together.

After researching and preparing their arguments, learners were invited, in a set of two pairs, to come out to the front to present their arguments for and against the dismissal of the TV celebrity in the style of a *Question Time* panel. One of the pair was charged with presenting the case and the other with answering questions. Learners in the audience were given a sheet to assess the speakers against the last three success criteria above. The students used the assessment criteria and gave good feedback on each learner's speaking and listening skills and how well they met the criteria. They were asked to comment on two things that were done well and one area that could be improved. Later, the groups swapped over, and the 'panellists' became the audience and completed the assessment sheets on the other half of the group. This led to some really good discussion of the speaking and listening skills between the participants and the assessors. Learners finished the lesson by identifying one aspect of speaking and listening that they will focus on and use in their vocational context of beauty therapy. They were asked to share this target with their beauty therapy tutor and look for ways in which they could practise this skill in the salon.

Why was this good differentiation?

» The tutor had good individual notes on the needs of each learner and more importantly used them to good effect, particularly to organise the pairings.

» Each learner had clear objectives and success criteria for the lesson and could reflect on these at their own level of detail, but with good coaching from the tutor to help them extend their thinking.

» The tutor had established a good culture of learners setting their own challenging targets for improvement and in this case completing their own electronic individual learning plans.

» Each learner had an individual target for improvement and was tasked to develop that skill in a vocational context.

Differentiation in teaching and learning methods

The two most common methods of teaching and learning that I observe are:

1. teacher-led questioning to the whole class;

2. learners completing worksheets.

Let's examine how effective these methods are in promoting differentiated learning.

Teacher-led questioning

In teacher-led questioning, the teacher asks a question to the whole group and either invites anyone in the class to respond or nominates a learner to answer. Either way, one of the most commonly used techniques would appear to be the least useful in providing differentiated learning. A simple adjustment to make question and answer better suited to differentiated learning is to have some method for all learners to answer the question set. These methods can include using individual whiteboards, which means that all learners are required to answer the question. If whiteboards are not available, plain white paper will serve as well. The nature of the questions needs to be given some thought, but most straightforward questions can be usefully answered using the whiteboards method. Learners can provide short answers, indicate whether they agree or disagree with a statement or even provide suggestions for the spelling of words.

Worksheets

The second most common method employed is worksheets, containing sets of questions, usually the same questions for all learners. This method is not best suited to provide opportunities for differentiated learning. All learners have to complete the same questions. A few slight adaptions can make it more suitable. For example, you could choose questions that are progressively more difficult. Most exam papers are set up like this. You can start from simple recall and go to higher-order thinking questions that require deeper analysis. Another way to provide greater differentiation is to have some prompts ready, perhaps in envelopes, to assist learners with the questions. The idea is to encourage learners to use the question prompt only when they have exhausted other methods such as thinking of alternative strategies or asking for assistance from a peer. This method encourages learners to choose their own level of support and can be enhanced by the tutor advising and encouraging learners when, and when not, to access this support.

Differentiation by choice

There are a number of other ways you can develop activities to allow for greater differentiation.

Allow learners a choice of how they present the final piece of work. The task can be the same. For example, in one session the task was to research and produce information on the planned refurbishment of a local castle, which was a popular tourist attraction. Learners were given the choice of how they presented the information. Some chose to produce a leaflet advertising the attraction; others chose to include the information in a presentation. Others devised radio and TV commercials and still others presented the information as a newspaper article, podcast or blog entry. The key is that learners were given the choice to present in the way that suited them best.

Try this

This section looks at a few practical activities you can try to promote differentiation. It is a good idea to record your thoughts on these activities and how effective they are. For example, you might try the activities with two or three different groups and compare the effectiveness with each group. Reflecting on the success or otherwise of the activities is a useful way of reviewing your practice. A suggested proforma for you to record your findings is provided in Appendix 1. Feel free to adapt it to your own situation.

A good way to encourage learners to evaluate the learning and at the same time have some idea of the different levels of progress made by each learner is to have an exit questionnaire. The idea is that towards the end of the lesson (but ensure that you leave enough time to make it a meaningful exercise) you ask learners to reflect on the learning in the lesson. This can be done with pre-prepared questionnaires or on sticky notes (that could be stuck on the door on the way out). The object of this activity is to encourage learners to think about the learning but also for you to gain information on the different levels of understanding in the group. This is good for differentiation in that it allows all learners to reflect on their understanding of the learning outcomes and allows you to see which areas have been understood and which areas (and learners) need more input and support. This way you can tailor some of the content of the following sessions to meet the needs of your learners.

Not all learners have to answer all questions. You could ask learners in pairs to answer one or two questions each. Giving them the choice of questions to discuss and answer will further individualise the learning.

In the following list are some of the types of questions you might include in your questionnaire or use as prompts for learners to answer on sticky notes. Feel free to add your own questions.

Thinking about what has happened in this session, answer the following questions.

» What really made you think?
» What did you find difficult?
» What did you find easy?
» What do you need more help with?
» What are you pleased about?
» What are new things have you learnt about this topic?
» When do you think the most effective learning was taking place?
» How would you change the session if we did it again?

Whatever learners produce (and they will need support in carrying out this self-assessment), make sure they see that it is valued and used. Make it obvious that you have read their comments and have taken them into account in the following sessions. Learners will not put effort into something they see is not being acted upon.

Activity

The following activity asks learners to work with percentages. Produce a chart like Chart B in the example below. Explain to leaners that they are going to develop their skills in working out percentages. In this case it is percentage discounts, but it could be applied to any situation where percentages are needed, such as opinion polls, the chance of rain or interest rates.

As an example, choose a figure in pounds to put in the centre oval. Let's say £750. Ask learners what they might be able to buy for £750. This can either be something general or related to their vocational subject. You might be surprised at some of their suggestions and this will give you an idea of their level of knowledge of the price of items.

Show learners one way of working out 1% of £750. You could use the method, £750 divided by 100 times 1 (£750/100 = £7.50, £7.50 × 1 = £7.50) so 1% of £750 is £7.50. Do the same for the other percentages.

» To find 5%, £750 divided by 100 equals £7.50, times 5 equals £37.50, so 5% of £750 is £37.50.

» To find 10%, £750 divided by 100 equals £7.50, times 10 equals £75, so 10% of £750 is £75.00.

» To find 25%, £750 divided by 100 equals £7.50, times 25 equals £187.50, so 5% of £750 is £187.50.

» To find 50%, £750 divided by 100 equals £7.50, times 50 equals £375.00, so 50% of £750 is £375.00.

You might ask learners to work out other percentages such as 75% using this method. This would be a good chance to invite all learners to suggest answers using individual whiteboards or pieces of paper. It will give you the opportunity to see how well all learners are understanding this process.

The idea of this approach is to give all learners one method to calculate percentages. Encourage learners to explore other ways you might calculate percentages. For example, some may realise that 50% is one half or 25% is one quarter, so you could divide £750 by 2 to get £375, which is half (or 50%). Others may see that 25% is the equivalent of one quarter and divide £750 by four to reach £187.50, which is 25% (or a quarter) of £750. The key point behind this method is to provide one reliable method that all learners can use but encourage learners to find other methods that they might find easier, and promote differentiation by providing a method for all but encouraging learners to explore their own.

Figure 3.1 Learning percentages

a) Example of a completed proforma for percentages work

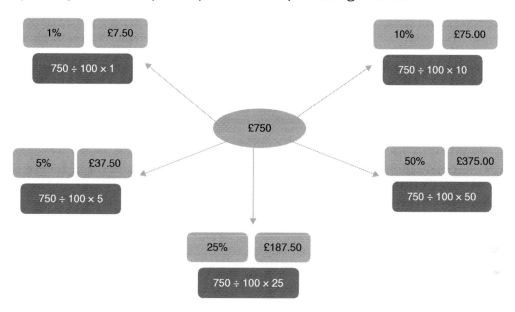

b) Blank proforma for percentage work

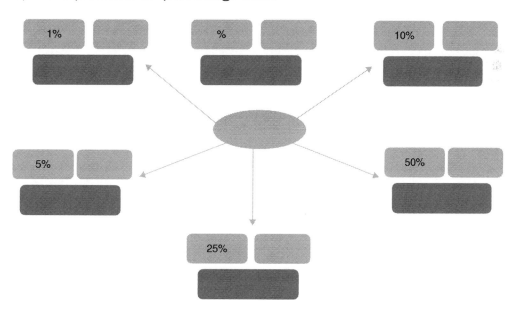

Summary (What should I do next?)

» Differentiation is about treating learners as individuals and tailoring learning to their individual needs.

» In larger groups individual learning is difficult but at the very least you should be able to deal with learners at the same level. Consider whether you are asking the whole group to carry out the same task regardless of their level.

» Knowing your learners well is the key to good differentiation.

» Monitoring the progress of learners will let you (and them) know whether differentiation is working.

Further reading

Miles, J (2012) Differentiation Without Extra Handouts: Tips for Stretching and Challenging Learners. [online] Available at: https://joannemilesconsulting.wordpress.com/2012/08/23/differentiation-without-extra-handouts-tips-for-stretching-and-challenging-learners/ (accessed 12 October 2018).

This is a very useful, short article about using differentiation in the classroom. It contains useful tips on what to do with early finishers and ideas such as a 'terminology box' where learners can choose a key word from the lesson and practise explaining it to other learners.

Petty, G (2018) Improve Your Teaching and that of Your Team: Differentiation. [online] Available at: http://geoffpetty.com/training-materials/differentiation/ (accessed 12 October 2018).

A very useful website with a variety of resources to use in staff development, including a mind map considering a range of strategies for using differentiation in the classroom.

References

Blatchford, R (2015) Differentiation Is Out: Mastery Is the New Classroom Buzzword. [online] Available at: www.theguardian.com/teacher-network/2015/oct/01/mastery-differentiation-new-classroom-buzzword (accessed 12 October 2018).

Didau, D (2011) Differentation: To Do or Not to Do. [online] Available at: https://learningspy.co.uk/assessment/differentiation-to-do-or-not-to-do (accessed 29 October 2018).

Ofsted (2018) Guidance – Ofsted Inspection Myths. [online] Available at: www.gov.uk/government/publications/further-education-and-skills-inspection-handbook/ofsted-inspections-myths (accessed 12 October 2018).

Petty, G (2017) Differentiation – What and How? [online] Available at: http://geoffpetty.com/wp-content/uploads/2012/12/0DIFFERENTIATIONwhatandhow2.doc (accessed 29 October 2018).

Sistemaengland (2005) Differentiation. [online] Available at: www.sistemaengland.org.uk/differentiation/ (accessed 12 October 2018).

Tomlinson, C and Allan, S (2000) *Leadership for Differentiating Schools and Classrooms.* Alexandria, VA: ACSD.

Chapter 4 Assessment for learning

> "*The term 'Assessment' is derived from* assidere, *to sit with or beside. It is something we do* with *and* for *a student, not something we do* to *them.*"
>
> **Wiggins, cited in Green, 1998**

Introduction

This chapter looks at assessment and specifically focuses on formative assessment. Assessment of learners takes place at most stages of the learner's journey. It starts with initial and diagnostic assessment and these are closely related. Initial and diagnostic assessment are processes carried out when learners first come to you. It is vital to establish where the learner is at the start of the programme; what they know and can do and what they still have to learn.

» Initial assessment is finding out about the learner as an individual including information about their background, their likes and dislikes, any special learning requirements and previous experience of learning.

» Diagnostic assessment looks more closely at the learner's strengths and areas for development in the subject they intend to study. It includes their current ability levels in English, maths and IT.

Initial and diagnostic assessment provide a basis to decide on the appropriate course and level of study for learners. Once this is established, the journey moves on and uses the two most common forms of assessment – formative and summative.

Summative assessment

Summative assessment appears in the form of end-point tests, such as end-of-unit tests or national external tests such as GCSEs or Functional Skills. These are infrequent, separate from the normal activity in the classroom and usually carried out at the end of a process. They focus on measuring achievement through a number or grade, which allows for classification and comparison between the achievement levels of learners. Their main purpose is to provide an easily recognisable distinction between ability levels that decision makers can use to grant or refuse access to the next steps, such as entry to further study, university or employment programmes. They are a blunt instrument and as such are not designed to provide detailed feedback on performance.

Formative assessment

Formative assessment is the opposite. The main purpose of formative assessment, or assessment for learning, is, as the name suggests, to provide feedback which can inform and shape the nature of future teaching and learning. Formative assessment happens all the time, both formally and informally, and it provides teachers with constantly updating information on what learners know, understand and can do. It's about finding out how well learning has taken place. This is the prime concern of any observer of your lessons. Their job is to make a judgement on the amount and quality of learning and progress that has taken place for every learner. This is the judgement you should be making all the time in your lessons. How do you know if learners have understood what you are trying to teach them? The simple answer is that you must assess their knowledge. The most common way to assess whether learners have understood is to ask questions. You have seen in Chapter 3 the danger of relying too much on this method.

Another common strategy is to circulate around the room and look at what learners have done and perhaps question or prompt them to show their understanding. This can be an effective strategy, but it is time-consuming and carries the risk of what other learners should be doing while you are focusing on one individual.

How can you measure whether somebody has 'learnt' something? How do you know when they have really understood and taken in some concept or practical skill? Think of something that you know how to do. It could be something simple like making a cup of tea. When you carry out this task, you know what to do, you are confident, you know the criteria for success, such as boiling water, the quantity of tea or tea bags, how long to leave it before pouring, even how much milk each person likes in their tea and how many sugars. If you know it well, you could probably make a good attempt at teaching somebody else how to do it, pointing out all the possible pitfalls to avoid. How did you get to this stage? You have probably forgotten, but it is likely that you were originally shown by someone or you observed someone doing it successfully. You probably tried it out under supervision so that you didn't scald yourself. It's a good bet that you made mistakes which you learnt from. In other words, you went through formative assessment, to build your skill and knowledge in the art of tea-making. Someone tasting your tea is the summative assessment.

A bit of theory

Effect sizes

In recent years there has been an increased focus on the importance of assessment as a means of improving learning. There has been growing emphasis on the clear differences between formative (assessment *for* learning) and summative assessment (assessment *of* learning).

In his book, *Visible Learning* (Hattie, 2009), John Hattie's research looked at 'effect sizes', as a way of measuring the effectiveness of different teaching strategies to improve learning (see page 15). Hattie's research showed that approaches that employ formative assessment techniques, such as effective questioning, sharing criteria with learners as well as self and peer assessment, constitute the third most effective strategy, with an effect size of 0.9. (An effect size of 1.0 is the equivalent of a jump of two GCSE grades, from 2 to 4; formerly a Grade E/F to a C.) This is why it is so important to get formative assessment right in your teaching and learning.

Black and Wiliam's booklet *Inside the Black Box* (Black and Wiliam, 1998) strongly emphasised the importance of formative assessment as a tool to improve learning. This short but very useful article is the result of a research review of over 500 articles and studies of assessment in education. It concluded with the following three points:

1. Formative assessment is proven to result in improving standards.

2. There is a clear need to improve assessment practice.

3. The key to successful formative assessment is the learners' ability to self-assess – an ability which must be taught and practised.

The study goes on to make valuable points about the negative effect of the use of questioning, where the learner's role seems mainly to be to guess what answer the teacher wants: what I would call 'guess what I am thinking' questions. The study discusses the negative effect of a classroom culture where the emphasis is on giving grades and marks and 'getting the right answer', rather than individual feedback, acknowledging what learners have achieved and setting realistic targets for improvement. The study also pointed out the fact that while the evidence for formative assessment is strong, teachers have been slow to adopt the findings of the research and apply it to their own teaching. It recommended that teachers be given structured support to implement the ideas of formative assessment. A later study took this recommendation and implemented it in the form of an action research project.

Another study, from 2004, built on the findings of Black and Wiliam and formed a research project, through the General Teaching Council. The project ran over two years and involved 36 teachers (12 each from science, English and maths) from six comprehensive schools in two local authorities. The teachers were asked to employ four key formative learning strategies:

1. Effective use of questioning that developed learners' understanding of a topic (rather than the 'guess what I'm thinking' questions).

2. Comment-only marking rather than awarding marks or grades.

3. Sharing success criteria with learners and ensuring that they understood how work would be judged.

4. Extensive use of self- and peer assessment, which encouraged learners to give and receive constructive criticism and advise others on how they could improve their work.

Over the two-year period, the attainment of the experimental group using these formative assessment strategies improved by 15 per cent, compared to control groups which did not employ the strategies. The results were published in a paper entitled *Assessment for Learning: Putting it into Practice*. Apart from improvements in attainment, the key finding was that learners moved from being *'passive receivers of knowledge delivered by the teacher, to active learners who were able to, and were expected to, take responsibility for their own learning'* (Black et al, 2003, p 4).

This outcome is a key factor in successful learning, and anything which moves learners towards this state should be encouraged. On reflection, the participants in the study identified the following key differences between teaching and learning practice before and after the project:

» the importance of encouraging more learners to participate in discussions by allowing all learners more time to think about their answers;

» viewing 'wrong' answers or misconceptions as valuable learning tools and creating a culture where it was acceptable (and even encouraged) to make a mistake and one where mistakes are seen as valuable stages in the learning process;

» asking more open questions to encourage higher-order thinking and discussion, rather than an overreliance on questions which only require recall of knowledge;

» monitoring learners' response to written feedback and clearly relating teacher's feedback to demonstrable improvements in understanding;

» regular use of self- and peer assessment, encouraging learners to comment on each other's work.

These key factors formed the basis of the change in teaching and learning that resulted in improvements. It is well worth thinking about how you might employ them more regularly in your own teaching.

From the files

The following real example shows less effective assessment for learning (case study 1) and a good example of assessment (case study 2).

Case study 1

In an engineering class in a general FE college there were 11 learners, all male and in the first year of the course. This lesson took place roughly halfway through the course. The teacher had set the group the task of identifying materials that might be supplied in different forms, for example in plastics, wood and metals. Learners were asked to work in groups to answer questions from a worksheet. The worksheet contained images of building materials such as windows, guttering, tiles and flooring. The task was to identify the different types of materials that each of these items could be supplied in. For example, are the windows plastic, metal or wooden?

Learners sat in rows and worked in groups of two and three, quietly discussing the questions and using laptops to research their answers. The teacher was circulating, talking to groups of learners to question them and check on their progress.

After 20 minutes, the teacher brought the class back together to go through the answers to the questions. The first two groups that were asked were unable or unwilling to answer the first worksheet question, so the teacher changed tactic and asked questions of the whole class.

The teacher asked a series of questions, including, 'What is in your house that is metal and is normally on a roll and begins with "F"?' One learner answered, 'foil'. The next question was: 'What is bitumen felt used for?' Nobody was confident enough to answer.

The teacher carried on with similar questions with most learners listening passively, and three learners at the back less interested, one of whom had his head on the desk. One learner asked why it was not healthy to breathe in dust and as the tutor was answering the question, three learners on the back table were talking among themselves. Of the three learners at the back table, two of them were on their phones under the desk.

The teacher showed a short video on how aluminium cans are made and after the video the teacher asked, 'Any questions?' to which the learners said, 'No.'

Case study 2

There were 14 learners present in a hairdressing theory lesson in a general FE college. The teacher had been with this group for 12 weeks. This lesson was a practical lesson on different styles of cutting hair, carried out in a classroom that was a well-equipped salon to industry standard. The teacher went through individual targets, listed against each learner and written on a whiteboard at the front of the room. He quickly checked that all the learners knew what they were working on in this session.

The teacher demonstrated a short graduation haircut on a model head, demonstrating different types of cut. Learners were asked to volunteer to come to the front and demonstrate a cut. One learner volunteered, and the tutor asked other learners to advise her on the cut, which many did. The learners discussed the cut with little reference to the teacher, who listened and came in with a few questions and suggestions to encourage learners to think more about their discussions. The first learner chose another learner to carry out the rest of the demonstration, which they did willingly. The teacher advised learners to visit a training website to access free training tutorials and most learners wrote down the website of the training videos.

All the learners had been involved in a salon assessment yesterday, where an external assessor came to the college to test the learners' skills in dealing with real clients. The teacher referred to this assessment and pointed out feedback from the external assessor on the professional behaviour and appearance of every learner. The teacher concluded by saying, 'Good to see that yesterday all of you had made progress. I am very proud of you.' He asked around the group for their feelings after the commercial salon assessment. One learner said it was 'fantastic'. The teacher then led a discussion which highlighted the skills that learners had improved, such as professional presentation and talking to clients, making a note of the key points on the board. Learners were engaged and involved in a discussion of a forthcoming hairdressing trade show and the teacher encouraged learners to attend, to improve their skills.

Learners moved to their own stations to practise their cuts and work on their own model heads. Each learner was asked to write down what skills they were working on and put it on a sticky note attached to the mirror. Some examples of targets were: cutting technique, getting the correct angle, accuracy and professional finish. The teacher went around and used these targets to start the conversation about how learners were progressing. For the rest of the session, learners worked hard, and the tutor circulated, supported and challenged learners to improve their understanding of their individual targets.

To conclude, the teacher used a multiple-choice quiz where learners answered on their mobile phones and the results were displayed on the whiteboard. This clearly indicated that all learners had made progress in their understanding of the key learning outcomes.

Key learning points

Case study 1 represents a common scenario. Learners have been given a worksheet to complete and asked to work in small groups. In this case they have access to laptops to research the information on materials. Most of them are working quietly, researching, discussing and writing down answers. Three learners at the back of the room are less interested and take the opportunity to discuss other topics.

Some questions to consider with this case study are:

1. Why are so many learners reluctant to answer questions? Do you think they know the answer, having worked quietly and apparently productively on their research?

2. If they found answers, why do you think they do not volunteer them?

3. What could the teacher have done to keep the three learners more focused?

4. How well do you think the teacher assessed the knowledge and understanding of the group?

5. How might the teacher have used the video differently?

The key feature of the session in case study 2 was how much the teacher had learnt about each individual learner in the 12 weeks they had been working together. The teacher was a practising hairdresser and obviously had the respect of the group.

Consider the following questions.

1. In what ways has the teacher made the learning individual for each learner?

2. Why do you think learners are so keen to contribute in this session (volunteering to come to the front to carry out the cut, talking to each other and advising on the cut), whereas they are not so keen in case study 1?

3. How has the teacher used events outside the classroom (the salon assessment and the trade show among others) to reinforce skills development?

Think about it

Reflect on some of your recent lessons. One way to review your practice is to become your own observer. Think about observations that you have had in the past and look at your own lesson as if you were observing it. Choose one lesson or part of a lesson to reflect on and record what you find. Some of the questions you ask yourself could include:

» What methods of assessment do I use?

» How am I going to measure the progress of each individual?

If you are going to use questioning:

» How many questions do I ask?

» What kind of questions do I ask most frequently?

» How do learners respond?

» Who answers?

» Are most of the learners volunteering to answer or just a few?

» How in-depth are their answers?

» How do I respond to answers, particularly incorrect answers? Could I have responded to an incorrect answer in a different way?

» What do the answers tell me about how much my learners have understood the lesson outcomes?

» How can I ensure that everyone has at least a chance to respond?

Try this

The most commonly used forms of assessment involve questioning, talking to learners and feeding back on their written work. These are useful ways to assess, when done properly, but if you only use these methods you are missing out on some important ways to vary your assessment and get learners more involved in assessing their own work. If you find that most of your assessment is either talking to learners individually while you move around the room or asking questions to the whole group, look at the following suggestions for assessing learning in a variety of ways.

Learner-set questions

Ask learners to set questions either for themselves or for others, to test how well they have understood the learning. Setting questions is a good way for learners to test themselves on how much they have learnt and understood. Stipulate that they must know the answers to the questions themselves before they can ask others. A good variation is for learners to write questions for the teacher. They don't have to know the answers to these questions! This can be used at the start of a new topic, such as 'Write three questions you would like to ask about this subject'. Ask learners to hold on to these questions and at the end of the session, review whether they have found the answers. If not, they can leave the unanswered questions (and any that have arisen from the lesson) in a box to be explored in the next session.

Target setting

Ask learners to set themselves targets for the session at the beginning. You can set some of the targets and ask learners to set their own personal targets. At the end of the session, you can give learners one minute to discuss or write down how well they think they have met the targets set by the teacher and the targets they set for themselves.

In-class targets

While learners are working, ask them to set a short-term target for the activity. Ask them to write this on a sticky note and display it. Look at the example in case study 2, where learners were focusing on practising their graduated cuts. Ask learners to write on a sticky note specifically what skills they are working on. This can be attached to the desk or a computer and can be an excellent way of quickly seeing what skills learners are practising. You can comment verbally on their progress, or better still, leave them a different-coloured sticky note with feedback on their progress.

What does good look like?

When setting learners a piece of work, discuss it with them and give them examples of good or outstanding answers. It can be difficult to find these, but if you use work from previous students you can start to gather a database of good examples. This can be a bit time-consuming but over time you can build a collection of good responses, and the fact that they are real examples from previous learners can have a really motivating effect. Give learners the criteria and ask them to 'mark' these answers. In this way they can become familiar with the success criteria, and at the same time have good examples of best practice.

Talk share

As part of a plenary session or to recap learning during a session, ask learners to pair up and discuss: two new things they learnt in the session; what was easy; what was difficult; one question they would like answered; and one thing they are confident they could explain to someone else. Have them record this information and let you have it or ask some pairs to report back to the group.

Question box

This is a good way to encourage learners to ask questions without the fear of appearing foolish. Ask learners to write a question and put it anonymously into a box, hat or some other container at the front of the class. Read these out or ask learners to pick out questions to read out. This way questions can be addressed without the need to reveal the questioner. Establish rules with learners to ensure that the anonymity is not seen as an opportunity to ask inappropriate or facetious questions.

One-sentence summary

Ask learners to sum up what they have learnt in one sentence, either at the end of the session or at intervals throughout the class. They can then work with you and their peers to share and refine their thoughts. (This has the bonus of reinforcing the use of correct sentences and concise writing.)

Instant feedback

There are several quick ways to gain instant feedback on the success of a period of learning. Among the most common is asking learners to indicate with their thumbs how well they have understood. Thumbs up means they have understood it fully, thumbs down mean they have not understood and thumbs held horizontally indicates that they have got some of it but are not entirely confident and would like more help. You can achieve the same effect with red, yellow and green cards to indicate: don't know; unsure; and confident. Learners can also give feedback briefly using individual whiteboards to indicate briefly how much they have understood. You could suggest they draw a smiley face to indicate they have completely understood it; a frown for still haven't got it; and a straight mouth for partially understood it.

RAG rating

Learners can review their work and indicate where they feel they have performed at their best. They can use coloured pens or highlighters to mark passages according to the RAG rating system (red = need to rethink this part; amber/yellow = reasonably happy with this but could improve it; and green = this is good).

Assessment criteria

Laminate some cards with assessment criteria printed on them. Have learners use them frequently during the session to assess how well they have met the criteria in their work. Encourage learners to work in pairs and peer assess each other's work using the cards.

Best work

Ask learners to find their best piece of work on a subject. Encourage them to explain to you and others why it is their best piece, and specifically what they have done well that they can replicate in other work.

Reflection logs

Develop learners' skills in reflecting on their own work. They can do this through a reflective journal, blog or video diary. At first, they will need a lot of help and a framework to structure their thinking and writing, but over time they can be taught to improve their skills of reflection and self-assessment, whatever their level.

Summary (What should I do next?)

» Review your planning and consider how you are assessing the learning of each member of your group.

» Ensure your learners are clear about the learning outcomes for each lesson. Find ways to engage learners in discussing and understanding the lesson outcomes, that go beyond just reading them out.

» Refer to the lesson outcomes frequently during the session.

» Consider giving learners good examples of work that meet the criteria.

» Think about how often and in what way you can assess the learning.

» Try using some of the assessment methods above, rather than relying too much on questions to the whole group or verbal feedback, to assess understanding.

» Review how much self- and peer assessment you use. Could you make more use of it? How will you ensure that learners develop the skills to self- and peer assess?

Further reading

Black, P and Wiliam, D (1998) *Inside the Black Box: Raising Standards through Classroom Assessment.* London: School of Education, King's College, London.

This short pamphlet is the result of a research review of over 500 articles about assessment and particularly the use of formative assessment. It highlights the importance of formative assessment to improve the effectiveness of learning. It discusses the importance of effective questioning and creating a classroom culture where learning is valued above grades.

Black, P, Harrison, C, Lee, C, Marshall, B and Wiliam, D (2003) *Assessment for Learning: Putting it into Practice*. Maidenhead, Berkshire: Open University Press.

This study took the recommendations of the Black and Wiliam pamphlet above and ran a two-year project based on the findings. It contains useful case studies of how teachers introduced formative assessment into their lessons and summarises the key factors for the successful use of formative assessment.

Hattie, J (2009) *Visible Learning: A Synthesis of Over 800 Meta Analyses Relating to Achievement*. Abingdon: Routledge.

This is the work of New Zealand educationalist John Hattie. It reports on research carried out over 15 years and more than 50,000 case studies looking at influences on achievement in school-age students. He assigns an 'effect size' to each strategy, such as questioning, group work, formative assessment, etc. Each strategy is measured on its effectiveness as a method of raising achievement and assigned a numerical value. Formative assessment comes out as the third most effective strategy for raising achievement.

Online

Erkens, C. et al (2018) All Things Assessment – All in One Place. [online] Available at: www.allthingsassessment.info (accessed 12 September 2018).

This is a useful resource from North America. It is a collection of articles and blogs on assessment in all its forms. Although it deals with school-age learners and has a focus on education in North America, a lot of the articles contain useful information that can be applied to post-16 education in the UK.

References

Black, P and Wiliam, D (1998) *Inside the Black Box: Raising Standards Through Classroom Assessment*. London: School of Education, King's College.

Black, P, Harrison, C, Lee, C, Marshall, B and Wiliam, D (2003) *Assessment for Learning: Putting it into Practice*. Maidenhead: Open University Press.

Green, J (1998) Constructing the Way Forward. Keynote address at Innovations for Effective Schools, OECD Conference, Christchurch, New Zealand.

Hattie, J (2009) *Visible Learning: A Synthesis of Over 800 Meta Analyses Relating to Achievement*. Abingdon: Routledge.

Wiggins, G (1998) *Educative Assessment: Designing Assessments to Inform and Improve Student Performance*. San Francisco: Jossey-Bass.

Chapter 5 Giving feedback

"There is no failure. Only feedback."

Robert G Allen

Introduction

Providing feedback to learners, whether written or verbal, is vital in the learning process. You spend a good proportion of your time commenting on learners' work, pointing out whether they have met learning outcomes and highlighting errors of spelling and punctuation. Add to this the amount of time spent talking to learners or questioning them to think more deeply and you can see how much time and effort is involved in giving feedback. The quality of feedback is key in making a judgement of how much learning has taken place. As this is the same judgement to be made by anyone who observes your lesson, it is clear that understanding how to provide effective feedback is crucial in any successful learning experience. This chapter looks at how feedback to learners, in three key forms (written, verbal and peer feedback), can be used to make learning more effective.

It examines research projects that have focused on learners' feelings about feedback and which types of feedback they have found most useful. In the light of these findings, I'll ask you to consider your practice and look at how you can make written and verbal feedback more effective. Of course, feedback doesn't only have to come from the teacher and so we will consider how to make the best use of the valuable resource of using learners to comment on each other's work, using peer feedback. The 'From the files' feature provides two case studies, one of which highlights good practice in giving feedback and one which demonstrates less effective feedback and shows the dangers of asking learners to comment on each other's work without adequate preparation. Finally, in 'Try this', I suggest some strategies to improve the effectiveness of each area of written, verbal and peer-to-peer feedback.

A bit of theory

What does the research say?

Relatively little research has measured the effect of teacher feedback on learners. Fritz et al (2000) demonstrated the key role of formative feedback and concluded that summative feedback alone, without any formative feedback, resulted in negative effects. Learners were demoralised by results, not having received any ongoing feedback to tell them how they were progressing. This emphasis on the importance of ongoing or formative feedback is supported by the research of John Hattie (2009), whose effect size research, discussed in Chapter 4, shows formative assessment and feedback to be the third most effective teaching and learning strategy in improving learner's achievement – quite a claim since Hattie identified more than 250 strategies that influenced the effectiveness of learning in over 50,000 previous studies.

Lizzio and Wilson (2008) surveyed learners' perceptions of the type of feedback they found most useful. You might not be surprised to find that learners value feedback most when it is:

» Developmental – that is, it shows them what they can do better rather than just what they have done wrong.

» Encouraging – learners need to be told what they have done well. This builds confidence and encourages them to carry on with their learning journey.

» Fair – learners need to perceive feedback as fair, including clearly stated learning outcomes that they are being judged against and clear reasons why they have been achieved or not.

» Demonstrating a sense of respect from teacher to learner that values the effort they have put in and gives a 'fair' assessment of their work.

It is essential that you look at any feedback given in the light of these factors and always strive to demonstrate them in your classes.

Weaver (2006) surveyed 44 students in the faculty of Business and Art and Culture. The survey indicated that learners:

» took more notice of timely and prompt feedback;

» found feedback useful but would like further help on interpreting it and making the best use of written feedback;

» generally found that markers' comments were too vague and could be more helpful.

What has observation revealed?

Although the following is a small sample, it reflects my own anecdotal findings from talking to learners and observing their reactions to feedback. The research also showed that there were four areas of feedback that learners found unhelpful. Learners said that feedback was not effective if it:

1. was too vague or general, using statements such as: 'good work' or 'try to be more detailed';

2. did not show learners clearly enough what they had to do to improve, using statements such as 'you need to be more precise';

3. focused too much on negative aspects of the work and simply pointed out errors without indicating any way to improve them; for example, pointing out errors of spelling and punctuation without suggesting strategies to improve;

4. didn't relate to any of the assessment criteria for the piece of work or reflected 'pet hates' from markers.

The research also found that feedback which explained why a certain grade had been given, and particularly what would be needed to achieve a higher grade, was more valued by learners.

The research concluded that learners require a balance of positive and constructive reinforcement. Overly negative written feedback can have a significant impact on learners' motivation and self-esteem. This is particularly relevant when correcting spelling and grammar. There is food for thought here which indicates that you need to reflect on how you mark work and ask yourself the following questions.

» Is your feedback timely enough to be effective?

» Have you been precise enough in your comments so that learners can really see where they need to improve?

» What is your strategy to ensure that learners actually do something with your feedback, whether written or verbal?

» Before you point out what learners have done wrong, have you found something to praise in their writing?

Bear in mind, also, that learners will receive written feedback from anywhere between 10 and 20 different teachers. If that feedback is wildly inconsistent it is little wonder that learners start to filter it out and ignore most of it.

A key consideration in giving feedback is the self-esteem of each learner. Confident learners may be better able to use constructive criticism, as opposed to learners with low self-esteem who may perceive any criticism as negative and demotivating and use it as an excuse to disengage with the course. It is vital that you get to know your learners and how best to motivate each individual.

Weaver's research also found that feedback was more useful when it was 'enabling' rather than 'judging'. In other words, learners respond better when they understand and see the purpose of feedback as a means of continuous improvement, rather than a series of one-off judgements. I see this all too often when feeding back to staff I have observed.

Discussing the quality of learning and talking through the strengths and area for improvement in an observed lesson can be going well, with the teacher fully engaged in thinking about the lesson and gaining insights and suggesting ways it can be improved – until we come to the grading. When a grade is given, and is not what the teacher expects, they can change mindset completely and move from involved participant to defensive apologists for the lesson, in an instant. At this point they begin to feel the need to defend their lesson and explain how factors outside their control affected the quality of the learning, or that much of the best learning occurred before or after the observer was in the room. This is a good example of the negative effect of feedback perceived as a judgement rather than an enabling discussion and is as relevant to teachers as it is to learners.

From the files

Case study 1

In a sports class in a general FE college there were 18 learners, all male and in the first year of the course. There was a mixture of learners and the topic of the lesson was speaking and listening. The teacher had set up a mock press conference, following a football match, to simulate a post-match interview with players. Three 'players' were chosen to be interviewed and the rest of the group were to play the part of the media. The three players had been given short scenarios to study (one was not playing well following a huge transfer fee; one was playing well and scoring although the team were in danger of relegation; and one was rumoured to be unhappy and wanted to leave the club). The room was set up as a media conference with the three players seated around a table at the front. Three members of the 'press' had been given questions to ask. The rest of the group were asked to give feedback on the performances of the 'players' and how well they answered the questions. Everybody was supplied with a feedback form which indicated what to look for when players answered the questions. These were closely linked to the assessment criteria for the functional skills speaking and listening unit. The remaining 15 learners had been divided into three groups of five and each group had a feedback card which focused on a different area of the speaking and listening criteria. For example, 'Give relevant responses in appropriate language'; 'Present information and ideas clearly'; and 'Adapt contributions to suit audience'. The teacher had discussed with the group the content of the feedback card and worked on ensuring each group knew what they were looking for. They had discussed how to give verbal feedback to stress the positives and to make clear one area where they could improve. It was clear that this was not the first time they had done this, and learners had developed good skills in framing feedback to be accurate and encouraging. They carried out a lively mock press conference. One player, when asked a question about the team's poor defensive record and his own good goal-scoring form, criticised his team members. Feedback on this comment made him realise his mistake and review how he might have answered the question differently.

Case study 2

Learners were divided into groups and asked to research a topic to present to the class. The class in this example was an access to higher education (HE) course on health and social care. The task today was to look at the history of health care in the UK and research some of the milestones in the development of health and social care, such as the founding of the NHS, as well as discussing key findings of influential reports such as the Beveridge and Acheson Reports. This was preparation for an exam question, which appeared regularly on their end-of-course assessment. All the learners engaged enthusiastically in researching the information, in preparation for a presentation by each group on their chosen subject. Learners were asked to present their findings on A3 paper and ensure that each member of the three-person group took some part in the presentation. Each group came to the front of the class to present their findings. They all displayed their A3 sheets, most holding them and some trying to attach them to the whiteboard. Everybody took some part in feeding back, while the rest of the group listened attentively. The quality of presentation was varied, with some speaking clearly and engaging with the audience and some less clear and reading the information on the A3 sheets without really explaining what they had found. A minority of learners spoke clearly and presented well but most read from the sheet or made little eye contact with the audience. The teacher asked the rest of the group to ask questions, which a few did and then asked them to feed back to each group. Most learners were unable to make any comments beyond saying that all groups had done well and the presentations were interesting. One learner commented that one person in one group could have spoken up. All groups received a round of applause and sat down.

Key learning points

In case study 1 all learners were clear about the assessment criteria and had a chance to discuss what they would be looking for. Learners were attentive and purposeful during the presentations, because they had clear assessment criteria to look out for and comment on. Much work had been done over time to ensure that learners developed the difficult skill of identifying areas for improvement and feeding back in a manner which did not aggravate or demoralise the recipient. The class used a format of 'What went well' followed by 'Even better if', which ensured a positive and constructive atmosphere. The teacher had reminded them all that at some point in the future it was likely that they would be the one being fed back to and to bear in mind the constructive purpose of the feedback. As a result, the exercise was a positive and enjoyable one.

Case study 2 is an example of an activity which is very common in my experience. Learners are asked to present their findings to the rest of the class and other group members are asked to comment on their presentations. Standing up in front of an audience of your peers is nerve-wracking and difficult, even for confident learners, and it can be an ordeal for those lacking in confidence. But so often, as in the example here, learners present and sit down without any real feedback on their performance or how it could be improved. It is difficult for a teacher or other members of the group to give meaningful and useful feedback on presentation skills (as opposed to the content of the presentation), but it is essential if learners are going to develop these skills. It is important that, over time, learners are taught to understand the key factors of a good presentation, such as: speaking clearly; making good eye contact; reading your audience; body language and posture (What do you do with your hands when presenting?). This has not been done here and while learners had had an opportunity to present, they could have learnt much more about presentation skills. Think about your own practice. Give learners plenty of opportunity to look at expert presenters and examine not only what they say, but what skills they use in presenting. Plenty of excellent presentations can be found, using resources such as TED Talks. Learners must be taught to look out for these things and, perhaps more importantly, develop the skills of feeding back in such a way that the experience is a positive one for all parties.

Think about it

The three types of feedback

Before you read the next section, think about the three types of feedback (written, verbal and peer feedback) and reflect on how effectively you currently use each in your teaching.

Written feedback

Look through the written work of two of your learners. You might like to choose one learner who has made good progress and one about whom you have concerns. Now look at their work from the point of view of your marking and written comments. What do you notice? Is there any difference in the way you respond to each of these learners?

Look through their work over a period of time. How have they responded to your written comments? Is there any evidence to show that either or both have improved their skills as a result of what you have written? If you had to prove in a court of law how they have improved as a result of written feedback that you have given, how strong a case would you have? If you are finding little evidence that your learners are reading, taking note and acting upon your feedback, think about how you can change what you do and look at some of the ideas in the next section.

Try this

Marking work

Consider whether you need to mark all learners' work to the same depth of detail. To mark every piece of written work thoroughly for every learner is a lot of hard work and particularly frustrating if you are not seeing any significant progress. You could choose one piece of work out of every four to focus on and mark in more detail. For three pieces of writing, read through learners' work quickly without annotating it, and indicate with a brief encouraging comment that you have read it. Keep a note for yourself of a couple of issues that you can feed back verbally to each learner. Perhaps one thing you think they have done well and one thing they should look to improve. These could include how well you think the learner has understood the task and also some note of the learner's ability to express themselves effectively and accurately in writing. These notes are a good source of information for you to build a personal profile of each learner's strengths and areas for improvement. When you give verbal feedback to the learner on this piece of work, make sure they make a note of one thing they can focus on in the next piece of writing. Get them to annotate the piece of work. In other words, let the learner become the marker of their own work. Ask learners to write a very brief summary of your feedback, highlighting one area they will focus on in the next piece of writing. You might encourage learners to mark on their work somewhere the aspect of feedback they have corrected and point you to where you can find the improved work in this next assignment.

For every third or fourth piece of work, mark it in more detail and let learners have a separate feedback sheet with perhaps two areas where they performed well and two you would like to see improved in the next piece of writing. Insist that learners write some response to this feedback, not only to ensure that they have read it, but also to state what they are going to do and how they plan to improve in the next piece of writing. Ask them to clearly indicate where you can find the improved work when you mark it. Consider allocating some lesson time for learners to review and correct work that has been marked. In my experience, allowing learners time in lessons to respond to written feedback is very rare but can have a significant effect in developing skills and reinforces the importance of responding to teacher feedback.

Verbal feedback

Consider the purpose of verbal feedback. What are you trying to achieve when you move around the group asking questions or checking on progress? Do you use a 'coaching' approach or a 'telling' approach? Let me explain. How many times do you find yourself telling learners the answer? How much time do you spend encouraging learners to find the answer for themselves, using phrases such as 'What do you think the answer could be?' Have you a plan to speak to learners of different abilities in different ways? How do you check that the advice you give to learners is taken on board? When they nod in agreement and say that they have understood, do you think they really have? How would you test understanding? Reflect on these questions and then look at the next section for ideas.

Try this

This is the most common form of feedback. You spend hours talking to learners about their work. Have you really thought about the purpose of all this verbal feedback? Consider the following strategies when you are feeding back verbally to learners.

Encourage learners to find answers for themselves. Adopt what I would call a 'coaching approach'. There is a strong temptation to simply give the learner the answer when they ask you a question. Try instead responding with questions of your own.

» What do you think the answer is?

» Where might you start looking to find the answer to this one?

» What would you say if you did know the answer?

» If you don't know the answer, what do you know about the subject?

» What questions could you ask to find out more?

This coaching approach can seem difficult and often learners will find it difficult to move out of the 'but you're the teacher and you should know the answers' mode, but stick with it and see what happens. To check that learners have understood your verbal feedback, you could ask them to briefly bullet point what you have said on a sticky note, or say that you will return to them in 10 to 15 minutes and ask them to recap on the key points of your verbal feedback.

Peer-to-peer feedback

How much peer-to-peer feedback do you use? How often and in what ways do you encourage learners to look at their own or other learners' work and assess it? What is the quality of the feedback that learners provide for each other, whether written or verbal? Are you happy with it? Where are the key areas to improve? How do you help learners develop the skills required for effective peer-to-peer feedback? Next time you have learners present work to the rest of the class, ask them to give feedback on the presentations. Judge how effective and useful this feedback is. It's a difficult skill to feed back to peers and provide useful feedback. Think about how you can make it a meaningful experience for the presenters and the learners who feed back. Think about this before going on to the next section for some ideas.

Try this

Peer feedback is a particular skill and learners need guidance and plenty of practice before they become good at it. But it is worth the effort. The ability to view another's work and feed back constructive criticism whether written or verbal is a valuable skill in future work. When learning to feed back, learners need lots of guidance and structure to frame their comments. They need clear assessment criteria and help in understanding what to look for when assessing.

If you are going to ask learners to give feedback on presentations given by other learners, be prepared to put in some work to educate learners how to do this effectively. Too often learners are asked to give feedback on presentations without any clear guidance or preparation. The result is usually some vague remarks that do nothing to improve the presentation skills of their peers. You might divide learners into groups and give them prompt sheets with things to look for, both in terms of content and presentation skills. For example, two or three learners could be asked to look at the content and comment on whether they feel more confident in understanding what the presentation was about. Could they summarise the main points after listening to the presentation? Other learners could be asked to look at presentation skills such as use of voice; eye contact with the audience; posture and body language of the presenters; or the usefulness of slides or visual material. For example, was it clear and engaging, could it be read easily and did it make sense?

Responding to incorrect answers

How do you respond to learners who give you incorrect answers? You don't want to squash their enthusiasm and make them reluctant to volunteer answers in the future, but on the other hand you need to make it clear that their answer is incorrect. There are a number of ways you can respond to incorrect or partially correct answers. Try responding like this.

» *'That's interesting. How did you come to that answer?'* Here you are asking the student to explain their thinking and with a few more questions you might find they arrive at the required answer themselves.

» *'You're somewhere near the answer but...'* This acknowledges that the learner has grasped some part of the answer (but only use it if they have) and encourages them to think more deeply to find the limits of their current knowledge.

» *'That's a useful point. Tell us more...'* This one is designed to encourage learners to think more about the topic and either expand on their point or ask for a volunteer from the rest of the group to carry on the discussion.

» *'Thanks'* (and move on without further comment). This is useful, particularly when a lot of the class want to answer. Limit yourself to simply (and genuinely) thanking learners for providing an answer and move on to the next person. Make sure at the end of this that you make it clear to the class what the correct answer is. You might also consider asking the whole class to discuss with a partner how their answer differed from the final one you provide.

» *'That's interesting because a lot of people think that is the answer; however, the answer is* (provide answer) *but a lot of people think like you did.'* This lets the learner down gently and avoids embarrassment by stressing that it is a common error.

One final approach which worked well with a group where the teacher and learners had a good working relationship was where the teacher responded to an incorrect answer by saying, *'Thank you. Everyone else should know that before the lesson, I asked* (learners' name) *to provide an incorrect answer here so that we can look at common mistakes learners make.'*

Summary (What should I do next?)

» Consider how effectively the feedback you give makes a difference to the work that learners do. Make sure you, and anyone else who wants to look, can clearly see the progress learners are making.

» Think about how you can prove to the learner that they are making progress as a result of the feedback you are giving them. Making progress can be a powerful factor when learners are feeling unmotivated.

» Think about the verbal feedback you give to learners; for example, when they respond to a question in class. Think about how you can make the best use of the verbal feedback you give to learners as you work your way around the classroom.

» Look at how effectively you use peer-to-peer feedback. Learners can learn a lot from each other and it is well worth investing time in helping them to become highly effective givers (and receivers) of feedback.

» Allow learners time in the lesson to review and correct their work under supervision.

Further reading

McVey, D (2015) What Makes Written Feedback Outstanding? [online] Available at: www.llnkedin.com/pulse/what-makes-written-feedback-outstanding-deborah-mcvey/ (accessed 12 October 2018).

This is a very interesting article from Deborah McVey. It considers what good feedback can achieve and how to make written feedback more effective. It has some good ideas for different opportunities to allow learners to develop peer-to-peer feedback skills, as well as quoting some examples of best practice in involving learners in giving feedback.

Naylor, R (2014) Good Feedback Practices, Prompts and Guidelines for Reviewing and Enhancing Feedback for Students. [online] Available at: www.researchgate.net/publication/266797954_Good_Feedback_Practices_Prompts_and_guidelines_for_reviewing_and_enhancing_feedback_for_students (accessed 12 October 2018).

Although aimed at giving advice to teachers on how to give feedback in higher education, many of the findings are relevant to work in further education. It gives a good overview of most of the major findings of research on feedback.

References

Fritz, C, Morris, P E, Bjork, R A, Gelman, R and Wickens, T D (2000) When Further Learning Fails: Stability and Change Following Repeated Presentation of Text. *British Journal of Psychology*, 91(4): 493–511.

Hattie, J (2009) *Visible Learning: A Synthesis of Over 800 Meta Analyses Relating to Achievement*. Abingdon: Routledge.

Lizzio, A and Wilson, K (2008) Feedback on Assessment: Students' Perceptions of Quality and Effectiveness. *Assessment and Evaluation in Higher Education*, 33(3): 263–75.

ThinkExist.com Quotations (2018) Robert Allen Quotes. [online] Available at: http://thinkexist.com/quotes/robert_allen (accessed 12 October 2018).

Weaver, M (2006) Do Students Value Feedback? Student Perception of Tutors' Written Responses. *Assessment & Evaluation in Higher Education*, 31(3): 379–94.

Chapter 6 Effective questioning

> *"I keep six honest serving men. They taught me all I knew,
> Their names are, What and Why and When and How and
> Where and Who."*
>
> **Rudyard Kipling**

Introduction

Kipling's quote reminds us of the power of questions in learning. The *'six honest serving men'* that he kept are the questions that *'taught [him] all he knew.'* It's a useful checklist when approaching any new learning situation and can inspire learners to have an inquisitive nature and develop habits of questioning, using this simple structure. Asking questions is a natural part of any lesson. It is probably the most common form of communication in any lesson. The path to effective learning involves asking questions. But who asks the most questions in a typical lesson? This chapter looks at:

» why we ask questions;

» some of the theory around questioning, particularly the use of Bloom's Taxonomy;

» how you can use the theory to plan effective questioning.

The chapter considers some of the features of learning where questioning is encouraged and what factors inhibit the effective use of questioning. Two examples are provided of lessons which demonstrate effective and not so effective use of questions. Finally, the chapter concludes with some practical strategies for questioning for you to try. When you try them, make sure you keep a review of what happened and how effective you think they were in your context. Use the form in Appendix 1 to record your findings.

Why do we ask questions?

Next time you're teaching, keep a note of how many questions your learners ask. Make sure they are questions from the learners and not just requests for further explanation of things you have asked them to do. Also, questions such as 'When does this session end?', 'When is break time?' and 'Do we have to do this?' don't count! Notice how many genuine questions they ask and compare it with how many you ask. What is the balance?

In general, teachers ask questions to:

» recap on learning from previous sessions and see how much has been retained;

» check understanding of new material;

» assess how much of the current learning has been understood;

» keep the flow of the lesson going and ensure that learners don't have to listen too long to the teacher;

» involve learners who do not seem to be engaged;

» find out the views and opinions of learners;

» give learners a chance to listen to each other and perhaps question and learn from each other;

» encourage learners to explore new areas of learning;

» allow learners to demonstrate higher-level thinking skills such as analysis and evaluation, building on learners' answers to encourage them to think further on the subject;

» help learners develop a range of important skills, such as interacting with others in a positive way (even if you disagree with them).

Questioning is a powerful tool to develop such a range of skills and therefore requires more thought and planning than you might always give it.

A bit of theory

In 1956 Dr Benjamin Bloom, along with others, published his theory of learning (Bloom, 1956). The aim was to promote higher-order thinking skills and move education on from simple recall of facts to more complex thinking skills such as analysis and evaluation. In doing so, he identified a hierarchy of skills – a 'taxonomy'. Bloom's Taxonomy has been adopted by educators ever since. (A taxonomy is simply a list or categorisation of any subject – think of the categories, or taxonomy, of animals such as mammals and reptiles.) Whether you are put off by the academic-sounding title or not, it is useful to consider different levels of thinking skills, particularly those related to what you expect of your learners when you ask questions and what types of questions are likely to promote different levels of thinking.

Bloom suggested that thinking skills could be divided into levels of difficulty, starting with basic recall of fact and moving on through several levels to evaluation, which he identified as the highest order of thinking. In Table 6.1 these levels have been related to the process of asking questions, so that for each level of difficulty there is the level name from Bloom's Taxonomy, some useful verbs related to the level, and some example phrases you might use for questions.

The difference between these levels of questioning, and particularly between knowledge or recall (which is the bottom of the scale) and the higher-order questioning, is neatly illustrated by an activity which is quoted here to show the limitations of relying too heavily on recall questions.

Table 6.1 Bloom's Taxonomy related to questioning

Level	Verbs to use	Sample questions
Knowledge Can you recall the facts? Can you name events, dates and places?	Tell, List, Describe, Name, Identify, Quote.	What happened after...? Can you name the...? What is the meaning of...? Tell me about...
Comprehension Do you understand? Can you compare, contrast, infer?	Discuss, Explain, Outline, Summarise, Interpret.	Write in your own words... What do you think the main idea of... is? Summarise the main points of...
Application Can you apply the learning? How can you use this information?	Show, Complete, Examine, Classify, Solve, Test.	Show how... Design a strategy for... Examine the role of... in... What would you do if...?
Analysis Recognition of hidden meanings. Distinguish between fact and opinion.	Investigate, Compare, Contrast, Explain, Arrange, Order.	What is the underlying theme of...? Design a questionnaire to... What else might have happened in the end?
Synthesis Generalise from given facts. Combine knowledge from several areas. Predict and draw conclusions.	Create, Plan, Devise, Rearrange, What If?	What would happen if...? From the information you have, devise a set of recommendations for... What else have you read that will help here?
Evaluation Make judgements about the value of thoughts, opinions and ideas. Recognise bias.	Select, Decide, Assess, Recommend.	Write a blog email report advising on change needed to ... Do you think that...? How effective is...? Do you believe...?

The Jabberwocky exercise

Geoff Petty uses what he calls the Jabberwocky exercise (Petty, 2009). He quotes a line from the Lewis Carroll poem, *Jabberwocky*, including:

> *T'was brillig and the slithy toves did gyre and gimble in the wabe.*

If you are not familiar with it, then all you need to know is that it is a nonsense poem containing words that Carroll made up. They don't make any sense. However, try answering the following questions.

1. What time of day was it?

2. What were the slithy toves doing?

3. Where were the 'slithy toves' 'gyring and gimbling?'

You could probably have a good guess. The time is 'brillig' and the 'slithy toves' were clearly 'gyring' and 'gimbling' in the 'wabe'. However, try this one.

4. How effective was the slithy toves' strategy?

This is a bit more complex. The first three questions lie on the bottom rung of Bloom's ladder.

They are recall question and don't require any other skills than remembering information. The last question on strategy required more analysis and a deeper level of thinking. This exercise neatly illustrates how the most frequently used questions require learners to do no more than recall information. They don't stretch them into thinking more deeply about the question. Consider in planning your lesson how many recall questions you ask and how many require learners to think more deeply.

Whole-class questioning

Whole-class questioning, whether open for anyone to answer or targeted at individuals, is the most common form of questioning that I observe. It has its place. It is good for quick recaps of knowledge or engaging those who are not participating or even in danger of going off task. (You should, of course, ask yourself why they are going off task. Have they been asked to listen for too long?) But it has its problems too. In a class of 18 or more, one person might answer the question. How do you know whether the rest of the class would have been able to answer? So often, and particularly when being observed, teachers pose a question and throw it open to the whole class. If the response is silence, the teacher being observed starts to get nervous and looks around for someone who is sure to know the answer. That person is called upon and duly answers. The teacher breathes a sigh of relief and moves on to the next question. The problem with this 'call and response' strategy of questioning is that all you know is that one person knows the answer (and probably has always known the answer). What about the rest of the class? How have you measured what they know?

Read the two case studies that follow. In the first one, the teacher has asked a series of questions to find out what the learners know about criminal law. Unfortunately, most of them are simple recall questions and most have been answered by the same few students. In contrast, read case study 2, where a much wider range of questions have been asked.

From the files

Case study 1

This was an access to HE course on criminology and law. At the start of the session, 16 learners were asked to look at a list of questions on the board. The questions included:

1. What is the name of the famous rule on insanity?

2. What does the case of Lewis tell us?

3. What does the case of Williams tell us?

The learners were keen and attentive and consulted their booklets to find answers to the questions. The teacher used targeted questions, asking one learner the meaning of the McNaughton rule on insanity (the answer to the first question on the board), which after much prompting, the learner answered. The teacher asked the question on the case of Lewis to the whole group and when no one volunteered an answer, asked one learner directly (one of the three who had been answering most of the questions anyway) and that learner was able to answer. Finally, the teacher asked a learner the case of Williams question. He answered fully and consulted his notes to refresh himself. For all of these questions the call and response method was used, with the teacher asking a question, one learner answering, and the rest listening. The whole-class discussion moved on to questions about definitions of sanity under the law. The teacher asked for the name of a condition and, when no one answered, said 'It begins with "E"' (epilepsy).

As the session went on, further questions included:

» What was Mr Lewis' medical condition? (The answer was diabetes.)

» What is the difference between hyper and hypo? (With reference to diabetes, too much sugar and too little sugar.)

» When might a person not understand the nature of their actions? (The teacher was looking for the answer 'diminished responsibility'.)

» What sentence did Mr Williams get? (The answer 'three years' imprisonment' was in their notes.)

» What year was the last person hanged in Britain? (1964.)

Case study 2

This was a session on travel and tourism at level 3. Learners were asked to identify the logos of ten large companies. They worked in pairs and questioned each other to find out more about the logos.

The teacher asked, 'What is competitive advantage?' A few volunteered answers and most showed that they had some idea of the concept. Learners talked about the concept with the teacher, who encouraged them to build on each other's answers. After a few minutes' discussion, most learners were much clearer about the meaning and application of competitive advantage. The discussion was characterised by learners talking to and learning from each other. The teacher only spoke to clarify a point, ask for further information or ensure that a few people did not dominate the discussion. The added advantage was that most learners had been woken up and energised by the inclusive nature of the discussion. Very few had chosen to sit back and take no part and those few who might have done this were quickly called upon to contribute. It was clear that this level of debate was commonplace in this session and that this had not been achieved overnight or put on for the observer. It appeared to be the result of long-term sustained efforts at building relationships and establishing the rules for discussions in that group. It was clear that this was what was expected in this class and most learners lived up to that expectation.

Following the discussion, learners were asked to work in small groups and were set the following task: 'Devise five questions to test someone's understanding of the methods organisations use to gain competitive advantage.' When all learners had their five questions, they were asked to pass one question to each of the other groups to answer. In this way most learners were able to see the questions from other groups and enjoyed trying to answer them.

Using targeted questions, most learners developed a good understanding of the features of advertising and how companies gather information on customers. The class split into two groups to look at examples of airlines (Emirates and British Airways). Questions they were given for research included: 'Who are their customers?' 'What products and services do they offer?' and 'How do they meet their customers' needs?' This research based on some guiding questions led to some interesting discussions between learners. For example: one learner learnt the term 'ancillaries' and could explain to the rest of the class what they are in terms of products and services provided by airlines. (They are the revenue from non-ticket sources such as baggage fees and on-board food and services.) Another learner found that British Airways provided a credit card, and this led the group to engage in an interesting discussion of the advantages and disadvantages of credit cards from companies.

Through discussion it emerged that some learners were confused by the difference between products and services. In this classroom learners felt confident to ask the question. The teacher clarified this with an amusing example (if you can take it home with you, it's a product; if you can't, it's a service), which he helped learners to understand.

Finally, one learner asked if you could take a dog on an aeroplane, which led to some frantic research and an animated discussion, with everyone involved in all aspects of the issue, including: 'Where would the dog be put when it was travelling?' 'How would it get food and water on long-haul flights?', 'What if a passenger is allergic to dog hairs?' All these questions came from learners. The discussion and the activity had involved learners in asking questions, and the pace and liveliness of the lesson had everybody enthused.

Key learning points

In case study 1:

» Almost all the questions asked were recall questions.

» There was very little follow-up when answers were given so that learners did not have the chance to explore the ideas further.

» Half of the learners in the group made little or no contribution to the discussion and did not answer any questions.

» All discussion was conducted through the teacher. Learners never had the opportunity to talk to each other in pairs or in small groups.

» At the end of the 50-minute session, only seven of the 16 learners had been involved in answering questions, and three had answered most of them. This meant that nine learners had spent 50 minutes sitting virtually in silence, taking in large amounts of information. Most of them were not taking notes; we can only guess where that information went, what those learners' feelings were, and how much they were looking forward to the next session.

Case study 2 is an example of a learning environment where questioning was a natural and frequent tool used by the teacher and, more crucially, the learners, to explore and expand their learning. Contrast it with what happened in case study 1.

All sorts of questioning strategies were used, including:

» open and targeted questions from the teacher to the whole class;

» written questions from the teacher to help guide learners' research;

» written questions devised by learners for other learners;

» learners asking each other questions to clarify their understanding.

» What are the factors that led to the creation of the classroom in case study 2, where questioning was shared among the learners and the teacher?

Some of the key components can be seen in Table 6.2. In contrast, I've listed some of the factors of a classroom where most of the questioning is done by the teacher.

Table 6.2 Shared questioning versus teacher-dominated questioning

Shared questioning	Teacher-dominated questioning
A variety of written and verbal questioning strategies are used.	Questioning is either open to the whole group or nominated individuals.
Questioning can start with the teacher but for a large part of the time discussion and questioning is between class members rather than always through the teacher.	Most questioning comes from and goes back to the teacher.
Learners ask more questions than the teacher.	The vast majority of questions are asked by the teacher.
Making mistakes or not knowing is seen as a valuable learning experience.	Making mistakes or not knowing is seen as failure.

Using key assessment questions

At certain points in the lesson you want to know how well you are achieving your goal of helping learners to understand the lesson aims. You don't want to leave this to the end of the lesson, by which time it will be too late to do anything about it. One way to check this understanding is through the use of a key assessment question. The idea of a key assessment question is to provide you with feedback on the general level of understanding among your group. It is a quick way to gauge how much progress learners are making. You need a question that will give you an idea of their level of understanding before you move on to more complex learning. Think carefully about the question. It needs to be worded so that everyone can provide an answer. Multiple-choice questions work best. Remember at this stage you are just trying to get an idea of how well you are doing in getting the messages across and how confident learners are in their understanding of the lesson. The key question doesn't test the details of why they know what they know, just the fact that they know it. You should set yourself a target, usually expressed as a percentage of the group who have understood the learning. This target will be different depending on the nature of the lesson. If you are recapping knowledge you have covered before, you may set a higher target, say 85 or 90 per cent of learners will demonstrate understanding. If what you are covering is new knowledge, you may be happy that 50 per cent of the group is still with you at this point! The key question will give you important feedback on whether what you are doing is working.

Activity

An example of a key question in a lesson on percentages might be:

A pair of shoes costs £60.
They are reduced by 25% of the advertised price.
How much do you have to pay for the shoes?

a. £30   b. £20   c. £45   d. £40

(The correct answer is c. £45)

All learners have to answer. They can use mini whiteboards or write their answer on a piece of paper. If you want to use an electronic method to get the feedback, there are a number of free applications, where learners can answer using their mobile phones, which can help to engage them in the process. The information you get from this answer will help you to decide whether the current methods are working; whether you need to review your explanation or spend more time on practice before you move on to more complex learning.

Pose, pause, pounce, bounce

This is a method of questioning attributed to an unnamed teacher and quoted by Dylan Wiliam (2009). It can be a good tactic to avoid the 'call and response' syndrome of the teacher and individual learners asking and answering a series of questions while the rest of the group look on.

Pose – This is where you pose the question. Think about a question that you can ask the whole class. It should be sufficiently challenging so that most people must think about it. This needs to be part of your planning processes.

Pause – Allow sufficient time for learners to process the question. This is the part that most teachers find difficult. Nobody likes silence and most teachers will break the silence within about five seconds. Avoid this. Allow learners time, say at least 30 seconds if you are asking them to answer individually and preferably more time to form their answers if they are working collaboratively. You can combine this phase with other strategies such as encouraging learners to work in pairs to form their answer or asking learners to give three answers on their own and at least five answers working with a partner.

Pounce – Sounds harsh, but this is where you nominate or ask for a volunteer to answer on behalf of themselves or their group. You need to think carefully about how you nominate or accept volunteers. You can do this randomly through a number of methods including lolly sticks with learners' names on them, assigning numbers to learners and randomly generating them through choice or simply by rolling dice. Another method is to ask the last learner who answered to nominate the next learner to answer.

Bounce – At this stage, pass the answer on to another learner for comment. Avoid the temptation to make any comment yourself or even give away in your attitude what you feel about the response. Simply thank the learner and move the question on to another learner to comment on, expand upon, agree or disagree with.

Activity

Using the 5 Ws and H

This is a very simple and effective method of devising questions for analysis, based on Kipling's *'six honest serving men'*, and can be applied to almost any new knowledge. The power of these six questions is that none of them can be answered with a 'yes' or 'no'.

Take an image or picture. Make sure it has enough about it to interest learners. Ask learners to form six questions about the image based on the 5 Ws and H. For example, if you choose an image with people in it, learners might ask:

» What are they doing?

» Why are they here?

» How are they feeling?

» When did they arrive?

» Where will they go next?

» Who are they?

In an applied science lesson, learners were asked to research the lymphatic system. One learner answered the question using this method of analysis and wrote:

» What is the lymphatic system?

» Why do we need it?

» How would we know if it wasn't working?

» When was it discovered?

» Where in the body is it situated?

» Who can be affected by it?

This simple approach to a new subject can be a powerful tool to start learners off and encourage them to think beyond simple recall of information.

Summary (What should I do next?)

» Plan your questioning as part of your session planning.

» Use a variety of questioning techniques in addition to open and targeted questions.

» Review how many and what types of questions you ask in class.

» Think about the participation of each learner in whole-class discussions, whether questions are targeted to individuals or open to the whole group. What about those who are not answering?

» Think about using a key assessment question to gain feedback on whether what you are doing is working.

» Ensure that you involve and challenge all learners with your questioning.

Further reading

Fearnley, P (2016) Questions to Improve Learning. [online] Available at: www.teachertoolkit. co.uk/2016/05/09/questioning-students/ (accessed 12 October 2018).

This short article contains useful advice on the kinds of questions to ask and the ones to avoid. It has a useful 'question matrix' showing how to frame questions of increasing difficulty.

Gast, G (2009) Effective Questioning and Classroom Talk. [online] Available at: www.nsead. org/downloads/Effective_Questioning&Talk.pdf (accessed 12 October 2018).

This is an extremely useful document from the National Society for Education and Art and Design. It brings together several strategies for developing effective questioning, promoting higher-order thinking skills and generally raising the quality of classroom discussions. It covers useful questioning strategies and suggests several ways to encourage learners to extend their thinking and questioning, beyond simple recall of information.

Liebling, M and Prior, R (2005) *The A–Z of Teaching Tips and Techniques for Teachers*. Abingdon: Routledge.

This book contains a lot of useful information, including discussions of what types of questions we as teachers are most comfortable asking and how much time we are comfortable to wait in silence, to allow learners to answer.

References

Bloom, B S (1956) *Taxonomy of Educational Objectives: The Classification of Educational Goals. Handbook 1: Cognitive Domain.* New York: David McKay Company.

Quotes.net (2018) Rudyard Kipling Quotes. [online] Available at: www.quotes.net/quote/1483 (accessed 18 September 2018).

Petty, G (2009) Improve Your Teaching and that of Your Team. [online] Available at: http://geoffpetty.com/for-teachers/questioning/ (accessed 12 October 2018).

Wiliam, D (2009) PPPB – Pose, Pause, Pounce, Bounce. [online] Available at: www.youtube.com/watch?v=TMBsTw37eaE&sns=em (accessed 12 October 2018).

Chapter 7 Embedding English and maths

> "*Bob, the talking sheepdog raced up to Farmer Jo. 'I gathered in 40 sheep,' he barked. 'But I only have 37 sheep,' replied the farmer. 'I know,' said Bob. 'I rounded them up for you!'*"
>
> **Adapted from www.mrbartonmaths.com**

Introduction

Hopefully you can find the funny side of maths, but development of maths and English is a key priority in further education today. Any observer of your lesson will have to make a judgement on how well learners are developing these skills. How can they do this accurately in the time allocated to an observation? Any judgements on the effectiveness of English and maths skills should be a judgement over time, not a one-off instance in an observation. Many people ask me whether English and maths should be included in every lesson. The simple answer is 'yes' but only if it is relevant. Don't feel that you must include activities to develop English and maths if you don't feel they are relevant to what you are teaching. There is nothing worse than teachers 'shoehorning' English and maths into lessons where they do not belong just to satisfy the perceived requirements of an observer. Few would argue against the need for good English and maths skills to enhance life, work and study, and currently four out of five adults have low levels of literacy and numeracy (that is, below Grade C/Level 4 GCSE) (Wright, 2016). At the time of writing, most learners are not achieving their desired outcomes in English and maths. To address this, current government policy requires those learners who have not achieved a Grade C or 4 in English and maths to resit the qualification, leading to a lot of negative feelings among students. Many influential bodies, including Ofsted and the Skills Commission, are calling for reform of this requirement to resit GCSEs and it remains to be seen how long it will continue to be implemented.

This chapter looks at how you can best promote the development of English and maths skills with your learners.

Why don't learners attend English and maths lessons?

Attendance at English and maths lessons is a problem in most organisations. Providers report real difficulty in getting learners to attend and the impact on observed teachers can be significant. If you have a class of 18 and only 12 attend, there is a real chance that the judgement on learning could be influenced by low attendance. No matter how effective the learning is for those who are present, the ones who are absent are not learning. How can a judgement of good or outstanding learning be supported if a third of the class is not there? Many teachers find this unfair, but this is the approach taken by external observers such as Ofsted. It is the joint responsibility of the organisation and the teacher to ensure that learners attend. Neither can do it without the support of the other and it is imperative that both work together to ensure that learners attend in the first place, and that once they are in lessons those lessons are interesting and engaging enough to make learners want to come back.

Several factors combine to make learners stay away from English and maths lessons. Some of the reasons include the following.

» Past negative experiences of English and maths lessons (including perceived 'failure' at GCSE), which means learners are unwilling to put themselves into a negative environment.

» Failure to see the relevance of English and maths. Learners typically say, 'Why do I have to do English and maths again? I came here to be a hairdresser, plumber, engineer, etc.'

» Lack of support from vocational tutors. Learners are much more likely to attend English and maths lessons if vocational tutors reinforce the importance of attending and emphasise how the skills developed in those lessons can be useful in a vocational context.

» Timetabling. It could be that the timing of English and maths lessons make it tempting for learners not to attend. For example, in one college learners had a three-hour vocational class on the Friday morning starting at 9am and then a three-hour gap to 3pm when they were timetabled to have one hour of maths. Little wonder that many of them did not hang around to attend the maths lesson.

The issue of attendance and achievement has given rise to several research projects focusing on the delivery of English and maths. Some of these are examined in the next section.

A bit of theory

In 2016 the Skills Commission published research highlighting the experience of students taking English and maths resits in further education. Figures quoted in that report are cause for concern. They include the following:

» Almost half of school leavers (46.2 per cent) do not achieve five Grade A* to C (or a minimum Level 4) at GCSE, including English and maths.

» The figure above means that, as the report states:

> *40–50 per cent of below average attaining students who do not usually choose to take English and maths qualifications under the optional retake system will now have to, and more of these young people will have to take GCSEs.*

(Mayhew-Smith, 2016, p 14)

» Figures from the 2011 GCSE cohort of school leavers show that FE colleges take more than twice as many GCSE English and maths resit candidates than schools and sixth form colleges combined.

In 2017, the Department for Education commissioned research to examine the delivery of English and maths in post-16 education and look at how best to engage this group of learners, identifying strategies that work in the planning and delivery of English and maths. The study looked mainly at general FE colleges but also included a few sixth form colleges for comparison, since results in providers with sixth forms are significantly higher than in FE. However, to put that in context, general FE colleges admit five times the number of learners who did not achieve A* to C in either English and/or maths, compared to sixth form colleges. Furthermore, five out of ten college entrants achieved English or maths Grade D/Level 3 compared to seven out of ten who entered a sixth form college. In maths, a third of entrants to FE college received a Grade D, compared to half of sixth form entrants. This goes some way to explain why sixth form results are so much better. The research sample included 16 of the top-achieving colleges and 15 colleges with the lowest rates of achievement. The aim of the project was to see what worked in improving English and maths outcomes for resit students.

The key factors in teaching and learning that successful colleges employ include:

» a variety of lesson activities that involve learners including active learning and peer learning;

» learning set in the context of, and related to, the vocational area. Successful colleges typically have classes made up of no more than two to three different vocational areas in one group;

» imaginative and innovative teaching methods that engage and enthuse learners, sometimes with elements of competition to motivate learners;

» frequent and justified praise for success, so that learners can see how they are progressing;

» breaking down longer tasks, such as exam questions, into manageable chunks and ensuring the learners fully understand before moving on to more difficult concepts.

None of these are particularly surprising. Interesting lessons that promote the relevance of English and maths in vocational areas, close monitoring of progress allied to frequent praise, and breaking learning down into manageable chunks, are key factors in any learning experience – and English and maths are no exception.

The following two case studies show examples of developing English and maths skills in lessons. Case study 1 shows effective practice and case study 2 highlights some common errors in embedding English and maths.

Case study 1

This lesson was a uniformed public services course. Eighteen learners were present, and all arrived on time. The tutor insisted on learners removing coats and having pens ready, which they did willingly, unlike learners in many other lessons I had observed in the same college. The teacher was enthusiastic and made good use of humour to engage learners. There was obviously a very good rapport between the learners and the teacher and I was surprised to find that he had only taken over the class six weeks ago.

Learners started by looking at a list of words on the board. Most of these words were new and challenging vocabulary for this group. The list included words such as 'apparition' and 'excavate'. The teacher explained that all these words would appear in a newspaper article to be studied in the next lesson and asked learners to write them down or take a photo of the board and look at them for next week's lesson.

The teacher had picked up from marking work that many of the class had issues with the correct spelling of homophones (words that sound the same but are spelt differently, such as 'there', 'their' and 'they're'). Learners were given a spelling test of ten homophones, most of which had been incorrectly spelt in learners' work. They included common mistakes such as 'where' and 'wear', and 'hear' and 'here'. He included the word 'bare' in the list. (An incident report used in the last lesson had described some football fans as 'bare chested'.) The spelling test began; however, the tutor 'accidentally' displayed the word 'bear' on the whiteboard. He later explained that this was a deliberate ploy to make a point about not copying off the board without thinking, and to make learners think about homophones. This worked extremely well in engaging learners and making them think deeply.

Following the spelling test, learners engaged enthusiastically in a card sort activity, where they worked very well in groups to make words from cards containing prefixes, suffixes and root words (eg un-success-ful). Learners engaged in heated discussion about the words and several learners were experiencing 'light bulb' moments, saying, 'I just realised "submarine" means going *under* the water!'

Case study 2

The lesson was part of a travel and tourism course. At the start of the observation I had introduced myself. The teacher knew that I was looking at the integration of English and maths in lessons and, while she could see how English skills of spelling, reading, speaking and listening might be developed, she was quick to point out, in our discussion, that she found it difficult to integrate maths into her lessons. She felt that the work she was doing with travel and tourism did not lend itself naturally to opportunities to develop maths skills. As we spoke, I noticed on the whiteboard behind her a note to learners about a forthcoming trip to a local attraction. The class was to visit and look at the way the attraction was promoted as part of the tourism of the local area. The note said:

The deposit for the trip to [attraction name] is due in by next Wednesday. The total cost is £45 and a 10 per cent deposit is required. Please pay before next week. Those who have paid, please let me have the balance before 30 May.

I asked about the note and she said, 'Oh, that's nothing to do with the lesson. That's a department trip'.

The lesson continued with learners researching information on a plan to upgrade an exhibition highlighting quite a famous local tourist attraction. Learners were asked to look at the proposed plans for the exhibition and suggest ways in which it could be improved. There was no requirement to discuss costing for the upgrade.

Key learning points

In case study 1, the development of English and maths was a key feature of the lesson. By the end of the lesson, most learners were clear about homophones and most improved their understanding of building spellings from root words, prefixes and suffixes. They engaged in animated discussions about creating words such as 'prehurt' (which they felt should exist!), and this discussion reinforced their skills of deconstructing and building words. Most learners contributed to whole-class discussions enthusiastically and asked a variety of questions to clarify their understanding of vocabulary. One learner was so motivated by learning a new word ('brawl'), that, armed with his new-found understanding, enthusiastically shared his description of a brawl he had recently witnessed following a football match! The teacher had succeeded in engaging learners and motivating them to take an interest in words and how they are constructed.

Case study 2 is a good example of a lack of awareness. The teacher had separated 'the lesson' and the everyday skill of working out percentages and calculating a balance for payment. When I pointed out the opportunity to practise and reinforce some number skills, such as working out 10 per cent of a figure and calculating the remaining balance to pay, she seemed genuinely surprised, as she had not thought of the information on the trip as being part of her lesson. In addition to this, when learners were researching information on the planned improvements to the local tourist attraction, there was no thought given to financial considerations of the proposed plans. For example, how much of a grant given by the local council (£2 million) should be spent on different aspects of the improvement plan such as buildings, technology and marketing material? The next section looks at how you might be more aware of opportunities to develop English and maths in your lessons.

Think about it

Reflect on your practice

There are three key areas which you need to consider when thinking about how successfully you can integrate or 'embed' English and maths into your teaching. I call them the three 'A's.

Attitude

Your attitude towards the development of English and maths skills in your lesson is crucial to its success. I have two T-shirts printed for my training. One says, 'Embedding English and maths – I *have* to...' and the other reads, 'Embedding English and maths – I *want* to...' Which one would you wear? I hope that you would want to integrate English and maths into your lessons. If you don't really believe that what you are doing is going to benefit learners, they will quickly pick up on this. The first step is to make sure that you believe that integrating English and maths is worthwhile and useful before transmitting this belief to your learners.

Awareness

The second 'A' is awareness. This is being conscious of opportunities to develop English and maths. Two types of opportunities will occur: those that you plan for and those that arise naturally. In your planning stage, look at what you are going to cover. Where are the naturally occurring opportunities to develop skills such as writing, reading, speaking and listening, spelling, vocabulary, or maths? It could be as simple as planning for a learner to read a passage out loud, or having a set of key words displayed, ensuring that all learners understand the use and spelling of terms that will be used in the lesson. For example, in a beauty therapy lesson you might list words such as 'sterilisation', 'hygiene', 'hazardous' and 'neutralise' and have a target for all learners to know what each word means, how to spell it and when they might use it.

If you know that your lesson requires some calculations, take time to ask learners how they arrive at the answers. Show an interest in the process of calculations as well as the answer. Make this a feature of your lessons, little and often.

You can apply the same thinking to unplanned opportunities that occur in your lesson. It could be a learner asking for a spelling or a realisation that most of your learners have not understood some part of the lesson. If a learner asks for a spelling, take a few moments to look at ways to find the correct spelling of words. Hopefully you might have dictionaries available or ask learners to look up the word on their mobile phone. Once they find the word, ask them to think about it and pick out something to say about it. For example, in a science lesson you may come across the term 'peristalsis' (the wave-like motion that moves food around the body). In this example, consider the prefix 'peri'. What does it mean? (around or near). How does it tie in with the action of peristalsis? (moving food around the body). What other words do they know that have 'peri' as a prefix? (periscope, periphery, perimeter). This can be done quickly and as part of your lesson.

Focusing on the make-up of words can reinforce their meaning, their use in context and their spelling. It can also greatly increase the chance of spelling other similar words correctly once you know the prefix. Being aware and encouraging an interest in words can be a powerful tool in developing learners' vocabulary and general confidence with language.

Activities

Once you have the attitude and the awareness, the next part of the process is the activities. You need some ideas to try with learners that will spark their interest and encourage them to be involved in developing their English and maths skills. These should be used little and often and can form the start of lessons or be used to summarise the learning. They need to be engaging and interesting, but most importantly they need to be meaningful and connected to the English and maths development that you are trying to promote; otherwise learners soon see them as gimmicks or time-fillers. Make sure you share with learners the purpose of the activity and which skills it is developing.

Try this

Ten things providers can do to improve English and maths results

Further education providers are charged with helping learners reach the standard of English and maths that many have failed to reach in school. And they must do so in far less time with far less resources. It is a difficult task, but some providers are faring better than others. In their survey, *How to be Good or Better* (Brown, 2017), the education consultancy firm FE Associates researched Ofsted reports published since the introduction of the 2015 Common Inspection Framework. From over 150 reports, they picked out the key factors that successful providers (those judged Good or Outstanding) have used to improve English and maths results. Adding their findings to my own experience, I have identified ten factors which are essential in improving English and maths results.

1. Full commitment and support from all staff, senior management, vocational and specialist staff

All staff must support the development of English and maths skills. It only takes one staff member when asked, 'Why do we have to do English and maths?' to reply, 'I don't know – just do it' to undermine a lot of hard work and effort. Even a teacher's subtle body language and attitude is quickly picked up by learners. You must believe in the importance of developing English and maths. Learners will soon pick up on it if your heart is not in it. Staff must be committed, and senior management must match that commitment in time, resources, marketing material and staff development time. Where and when English and maths is timetabled will tell you a lot about its relative importance in the organisation.

2. Focus on attendance

Good providers focus on getting learners into English and maths classes. They remove barriers such as timetabling and start times and use a combination of sanctions and rewards. Sanctions can include close monitoring of attendance; phone calls or texts to learners who are absent; talking to parents and carers to enlist their help; and, in one college, denying access to non-attenders by blocking admission badges. In another college each member of the six-person senior management team (including the principal) is allocated five non-attending learners, to monitor their attendance and encourage them to attend regularly. This way, 35 of the most persistent non-attenders are targeted, with positive results on overall attendance. Rewards can include prizes and formal recognition for full attendance as well as class rewards for groups with the best attendance records. The award of a 'bendy alarm clock' to learners with the best attendance proved to be a powerful motivating factor in one college. In 2018, research commissioned by the Department for Business and Skills (BIS) and carried out by the Behavioural Insights Team (BIT) found that texting updates to learners' friends and family about their progress in their maths and English courses improved attendance rates by 4 per cent, from 63 to 67 per cent and improved achievement rates by 6 percent, from 22 to 28 per cent.

3. Use the results of initial and diagnostic assessment to plan learning for each individual

Failing to use the results of initial assessment effectively is the most common area for improvement in many Ofsted reports. Initial and diagnostic assessment, if carried out correctly, can provide valuable information on a learner's ability. Use the results to identify the relevant strengths and areas for improvement for each of your learners and build in some development of these skills. Make sure that the results of initial and diagnostic testing are built into your planning process and monitor the progress of skills development alongside the development of vocational skills.

4. Vocational staff are clear about their role and work closely with specialist staff

If staff are being asked to embed English and maths skills into their teaching, do they know what it is and why they are doing it? Do they have an idea of what outstanding embedding of English and maths looks like? Do they understand that the only purpose of embedding is to develop skills? If staff are embedding English and maths and learners are not developing those skills, then they are wasting their time. Are there enough opportunities for communication between vocational and specialist English and maths staff? Close co-operation between all staff is essential. This way learners receive a consistent message about the importance of English and maths.

5. Learners understand the importance of developing English and maths

Do learners know why they are doing English and maths? Do you sell the importance of these vital employability skills? Talk to students. Explain how improving English and maths can benefit vocational learning. For example, learners could be asked to find out where percentages, fractions or knowing the difference between fact and opinion appear in their vocational area.

Helping learners realise the importance of developing English and maths skills is crucial. If it is not done, then you will have learners responding like this. I asked some learners the question, 'How does studying English and maths help you in your vocational subject?'

Here are some of their answers:

'It doesn't. We have to do it because we failed it at school.'

'It doesn't. I think we had a spare hour to fill.'

And my personal favourite:

'I don't know. I think we have to study them because it's the law!'

6. Strategies to encourage involvement and active learning

Once learners attend English and maths lessons, it is essential that they have an experience that makes them want to come back. Often you are fighting against many years of negative experience at schools. It is essential that English and maths lessons at college do not repeat that experience. You need to constantly keep learners involved and active. Sell English and maths skills; justify why learners should develop these skills and how they are relevant to vocational learning, further study and life skills. Any exercise that you do such as starter activities, word search, card-matching exercises, presentations or writing tasks – be prepared to answer the question, 'Why are we doing this and what skills are we trying to develop?' Be very clear about the answer and share it clearly and frequently with learners. Encourage independent learning to reinforce skills outside the class-room. (See the 'Further reading' section for a sample of self-study-based material.) Be prepared to do some work in class to introduce learners to resources that you expect them to study on their own.

7. Displays around college and in class support the development of English and maths skills (and staff refer to them)

How visible is maths and English in your organisation? In some providers, all staff wear a badge stating 'I ♥ English and maths'. Does it make a difference? Probably not on its own, but as part of a visible display of commitment, I think it contributes. I see plenty of examples of posters on classroom walls and around providers' premises, but what use do staff make of them? Have a look at an English and maths poster on the wall. When was the last time you referred learners to that poster? It's essential that all resources that support the development of English and maths skills are utilised as much as possible. For example, if a learner is having a problem with spelling or punctuation, ask them to take a photo of a poster that can help them remember and refer to it in their future writing.

8. Staff can share good practice in developing learners' and their own English and maths skills

Consider your own organisation. Are there enough opportunities in meetings, online, and through peer observation for staff to share best practice? It's easy to become isolated and feel that you are fighting a lone battle to promote English and maths skills. Higher-level English and maths skills are difficult. If staff are to help learners develop these skills, then they must be given enough time and support to help them carry out that development.

9. Know your learners' areas of strength and weaknesses

Do you know your learners' strengths and weaknesses? Look at your learners' written work. Are the same mistakes appearing repeatedly? You need to understand the areas where each individual learner needs to improve. Do you include development targets for English and maths on individual learning plans? Can learners see clear evidence of improvement? Improvement is a powerful motivating factor. Can you demonstrate that learners are improving in their use of English and maths? – most importantly to the learner themselves. Knowing and targeting individual areas for improvement is one of the most powerful ways to keep learners interested and engaged. As a colleague of mine says, 'Learning is a game; if you are winning you carry on, if you are losing, you give up.' Our job is to turn losers into winners.

10. Teach exam techniques

The surest way to succeed in examinations is to have a good understanding and a thorough knowledge of the subject, but additionally it is important to make learners aware of exam techniques and understand how their answers will be judged. As exam time approaches it is useful for learners to have plenty of practice at exam questions, for example, working out answers together; referring to mark schemes; and practising techniques such as demonstrating reverse calculations and showing working out.

Summary (What should I do next?)

» Understand the purpose of 'embedding' English and maths. The only reason to embed English and maths is to help learners develop their skills. If you are embedding and learners are not developing, you are wasting your time.

» Development of English and maths skills is not something you do only when you are being observed. It should be an integral part of your teaching. Little and often.

» Know your learners. Know their individual strengths and areas for improvement in English and maths. Praise their strengths and work on their areas for improvement, showing them clear evidence of their improvement.

» Include development of English and maths as an integral part of what you do in every lesson. Discuss words, think about calculations and how learners arrive at answers. Show an interest and reinforce the importance of developing English and maths skills in vocational areas.

» Look at your lessons. Where are the naturally occurring opportunities to develop English and maths skills? What will you do to address unplanned opportunities for development?

Further reading

Education and Culture DG. EU (2013) International Project on Maths in Vocational Areas. [online] Available at: https://sites.google.com/site/leovetmaths/ (accessed 12 October 2018).

The result of an international collaboration between educational organisations in Scotland, Finland, the Netherlands and Denmark, this site contains a lot of material including lesson plans, games and puzzles to promote the development of maths in vocational learners.

Bolton College (nd) Mathseverywhere. [online] Available at: www.mathseverywhere.org.uk (accessed 12 October 2018).

Available as a mobile phone application, this free app has useful videos on a series of maths concepts. Other features include facilities to convert between units of measurement and short tests to assess your progress. Funding for the app has stopped, so there are some features that do not work, but it is well worth introducing to your learners.

FE News (2018) The Importance of Embedding English and Maths into College Life. [online] Available at: www.fenews.co.uk/featured-article/16593-how-we-embed-maths-and-english-into-hsdc-college-life (accessed 12 October 2018).

This is an interesting article on how one college addressed the issues of poor attendance and achievement in English and maths.

Online

There are several sites where learners and teachers can find materials to support the development of English and maths skills. Among the most useful are:

www.bbc.co.uk/skillswise
A site from the BBC in the UK. Very useful for a wide range of resources to support English and maths.

https://misterwootube.com

Australian maths teacher Eddie Woo provides videos on a range of maths topics, mostly aimed at GCSE level but also provides some useful videos on functional maths skills.

www.mrbartonmaths.com

Craig Barton is a maths teacher who has produced a wealth of maths resources on this website. You must register for the site, but it is worth it for the resources, including maths worksheets and even maths jokes.

References

Brown, E (2017) How to Be Good or Better. [online] Available at: www.fea.co.uk/Media/Ofsted%20-%20being%20good%20or%20better.pdf (accessed 12 October 2018).

Mayhew-Smith, P (2016) Spotlight on... Young People with Below Average Academic Attainment and the Skills Sector. [online] Available at: www.policyconnect.org.uk/sc/sites/site_sc/files/report/448/fieldreportdownload/finaldraftsep16.pdf (accessed 12 October 2018).

Wright, D (2016) 5 Million Adults Lack Basic Literacy and Numeracy Skills. [online] Available at: www.jrf.org.uk/press/5-million-adults-lack-basic-literacy-and-numeracy-skills (accessed 12 October 2018).

Chapter 8 Promoting equality and diversity

> *"Everyone is a genius, but if you judge a fish by its ability to climb a tree, it will spend its life thinking it is stupid."*
>
> **Kelly (2004), attributed to Albert Einstein**

Introduction

The quote above, attributed to Einstein, makes the point that equality is not about treating everybody the same, but treating people according to their individual needs. Unionlearn defines equality and diversity as follows:

> *"Equality is about ensuring everybody has an equal opportunity and is not treated differently or discriminated against because of their characteristics."*
>
> *"Diversity is about taking account of the differences between people and groups of people and placing a positive value on those differences."*
>
> **(Unionlearn, 2018)**

Observers judge how well equality and diversity are promoted in your lesson. This is a difficult task when the observer might be present for only 10 to 50 minutes at the most. If there is no obvious opportunity to promote equality and diversity within the observation period, the observer still has to make a judgement. So, what can they do? They may question learners to see what they know. This is quite a skill given the constraints of time and some learners' reluctance to talk to what they see as 'inspectors'. The skilful observer asks questions and judges whether learners feel their individual needs are met and they feel welcome and comfortable at the provider. If there is no opportunity to talk to learners during the observation, a post-observation discussion will explore how equality and diversity are promoted. It is important that the promotion of equality and diversity is an integral part of your teaching and learning. It will not work if it is seen as a 'bolt on' or additional task which only happens during observations. This kind of 'box-ticking' approach does not benefit anyone. Equality and diversity should be part of what you do all the time.

This chapter looks at the Equality Act of 2010 and how it should impact your teaching and learning. It looks at ways to promote equality and diversity using group profiles. There is a discussion of unconscious bias and how to recognise and address this. Following an examination of some case studies, the chapter concludes with advice on handling inappropriate comments made by learners.

Equality Act of 2010

The Equality Act of 2010 placed a legal obligation on all education providers to protect against discrimination on the grounds of nine 'characteristics'. These are:

» age;

» disability;

» gender reassignment;

» marriage and civil partnership;

» pregnancy and maternity;

» race;

» religion and belief;

» sex;

» sexual orientation.

The act refers to these as 'protected characteristics' and you and your learners are expected to have knowledge of them.

The Common Inspection Framework of 2018 judges how effectively providers 'promote' equality and 'raise awareness' of diversity. But how can you do this?

How do you promote equality?

You can promote equality by:

» taking opportunities to highlight and discuss issues, such as examples of stereotyping;

» discussing current events that highlight where discrimination or prejudice have happened;

» discussing where action has been taken to ensure equality of opportunity.

Group profiles

A group profile is a good way of ensuring that you are aware of the needs of each learner. Brief notes on each learner could include any identified individual needs, ranging from a requirement for coloured overlays to how each learner responds in group discussion and which groups enable them to make the most progress. Awareness of each learner, built up over time and added to, will ensure that you are providing the best for each individual. A learner's profile can include:

» information about a learner's interests, skills, strengths and areas for improvement;

» potential barriers to learning and any additional learning needs;

» how the learner learns best;

» how they react when they are upset or under stress and how best to handle these situations;

» how they like to ask for help and what methods work best when providing that help.

Used successfully learner profiles can:

» help build relationships with learners;

» give learners an opportunity to talk about who they are, their past experiences and any assumptions that may have been made about them in the past;

» enable learners to talk about their aspirations;

» enable learners with additional needs to have input on how they would like to be treated and how best to overcome any physical or mental barriers to learning.

Why should you promote equality and diversity?

Promoting equality and diversity in your teaching and learning can:

» create a learning atmosphere where all learners feel their views are valued;

» encourage learners to feel free to express their opinions and voice their uncertainties without fear of ridicule. This leads to much more effective learning;

» help learners become more aware of stereotypes, discrimination, harassment and prejudice and so minimise the effects of these;

» help learners to understand why discrimination and prejudice may occur;

» equip learners with strategies to challenge discrimination against themselves and others.

Additional notes on learners can also be useful for observers. I once read on a group profile that one learner was liable to be volatile and prone to swearing and walking out of the class. The teacher noted that this was only for a short time and that the learner would return to the class. This helped me enormously when halfway through the lesson this happened. I was far better prepared than I would have been without the class profile! Group profiles, regularly updated, can be a valuable tool in treating each learner as an individual and ensuring real equality of opportunity.

A bit of theory

It is easy to assume that discrimination and prejudice can be a conscious decision. People may choose to discriminate against others based on characteristics such as the colour of their skin, or their gender. Fortunately, this type of open discrimination is rare in further education. However, we regularly demonstrate unconscious bias. This is bias we have as a result of our experiences and environment, which we may not be aware of.

What is unconscious bias?

The Equality Challenge Unit (ECU, 2018) states:

"Unconscious bias happens by our brains making incredibly quick judgments and assessments of people and situations without us realising. Our biases are influenced by our background, cultural environment and personal experiences. We may not even be aware of these views and opinions or be aware of their full impact and implications."

(ECU, 2018)

This section discusses the unconscious bias that we all have and how it can affect your interactions with learners. Human beings experience events and form memories throughout their lives. These moments are stored away in our subconscious for future use. In certain situations, we call on these memories to make decisions. In our primitive past it was an essential defence mechanism. We had to make snap decisions to judge whether some new or strange person or animal was safe or dangerous. We often reverted to judging whether they were 'like us' and therefore probably friendly or 'not like us' and potentially a threat, prompting the 'fight or flight' response. This was an essential tool for our survival. All the memories from our environment go to form our views and opinions. The explosion of mass media through forms such as advertising also contributes to forming our opinions.

Ross (2008) notes that scientists estimate that we process around 11 million items of information a day but only have capacity to focus on about 40 items! We deal with this by filtering out information based on what we like and what we want to pay attention to, often things that are like us or interest us. For example, if you and your partner are expecting a child, how much more do you notice other pregnant women? If you are thinking about buying a new car, how often do you notice the same model of car in the street? We are 'hard wired' to recognise and accept things that we are comfortable with and filter out things that do not fit in with our view of the world. This is what is happening in the learning situation all the time. We lean towards the preferences that have been shaped by our environment and upbringing.

The good news is that this unconscious bias can be addressed. You can lessen its effect if you accept that:

» we all have it;

» it is not a conscious decision to discriminate or be prejudiced against certain groups or individuals;

» it's more likely to be evident when you are stressed or hurried;

» it is a natural instinct;

» trying to suppress it may actually make it worse;

» you can do something about it.

To lessen the effect:

» recognise and accept that it will happen;

» acknowledge when it occurs – for example, when I mentioned a doctor why did I say 'he'?

» use examples of unconscious bias as a basis for discussion and an opportunity to raise awareness of the issues;

» include it, little and often and make it a natural part of your teaching and learning.

From the files

In the following examples, case study 1 shows how equality and diversity has been successfully embedded in the lesson and case study 2 highlights missed opportunities to raise awareness.

Case study 1

In a travel and tourism class the teacher explained the task: 'I would like you to work in pairs to cost a two-week holiday for a family of four. They want to go a warm destination with a beach.' She continued, 'Just before you start, can I ask you what you understand by the term "a family of four"'. The class paused and most answered, 'A father and mother and two children?' The teacher replied, 'Is that the only make-up of a family of four?' One learner replied, 'It could be a mum and three kids'. Another said, 'or a dad and three kids'. Others said, 'it could be mum and grandmother and two kids, or two mums and two kids'. Another added, 'it could be two dads and two kids'. 'Great', said the teacher, 'now what might be the consequences of assuming the family of four meant a mother and father and two children?'

Case study 2

In a training session on sales techniques, where the 15 learners were all female, the male teacher always referred to the customers as 'he'. Likewise, when giving examples of actions taken by the managers of the firm he exclusively referred to them as 'he'. Interestingly, when he mentioned office staff or admin support, all his examples referred to 'she'.

In his PowerPoint presentation several images were presented. They included: a woman washing dishes watching a man through the window mowing the lawn and a woman at the breakfast table feeding young children while a man with a briefcase walked out of the door.

Key learning points

In the first example of case study 1, the teacher had made good use of a planned opportunity to raise awareness of how we automatically make assumptions about people. The teacher had built this in very naturally to the task and took the opportunity to discuss how we assume details from the phrase 'a family of four'. She also went on to relate it to the vocational area by discussing the consequences of making that assumption and the importance of making the customers feel comfortable.

In case study 2, the trainer has reinforced gender stereotypes in sales by referring to the customers and managers as 'he', even though his audience was exclusively female. He has compounded this by giving examples of office and support staff as 'she'. In discussions afterwards, he said that he was not aware of doing this. He felt that if he was in the same situation again, he would take the opportunity to discuss briefly why he was using those stereotypes and how these assumptions might affect customer relations.

The images shown in the presentation also reinforced stereotypical male and female roles. There was an opportunity to raise this issue, perhaps by asking learners what they noticed about the images and open a discussion about stereotypes. However, this opportunity was not taken.

Think about it

Dealing with inappropriate comments

Learners sometimes make comments that are inappropriate. What should you do and how can you respond in these situations? You are certainly expected to acknowledge this type of comment, whether you deal with it at the time or note it and deal with it later. Learners' comments are often tied in with their view of the world and their identity. You must use your professional judgement and handle it with extreme care. The one thing you can't do is ignore it. Your job is to raise awareness and ask learners to question the way they think and the language they use. Doing this successfully without antagonising or alienating learners is an advanced skill, but one you must develop. You know your learners best and how you handle statements will rely on your professional judgement and your knowledge of each learner. Avoid becoming involved in long drawn-out discussions with one or more learners who may only be saying these things for effect.

Judge if that is the case and cut short the conversation if you feel that it is taking time away from learning. Remember also that creating an atmosphere in your learning sessions where learners can discuss possibly controversial topics in a balanced and mature manner will take time and effort, but it will be one of the most important life lessons that you can teach.

The first published research on the topic of how to challenge inappropriate comments was carried out in 1950 for the Commission on Community Interactions (CCI) led by Kurt Lewin to address racial prejudice, and particularly anti-Jewish remarks, following the Second World War. In this research, participants watched scenarios of differing ways to deal with inappropriate prejudicial comments. Later they were asked to judge which were the most effective ways of dealing with the comments. Plous, citing the research by Citron et al (1950), noted that:

> "the type of response seen as most effective was a calm, quiet objection based on (shared) values (e.g., fairness... teamwork)... 80% of participants preferred any type of objection to silence."
>
> **(Plous, 2000, p 198)**

This still holds true today. The best way to deal with inappropriate remarks is to stay calm and not react emotionally to the statement. Think carefully and plan how you will respond to inappropriate comments. It is hard to do when caught by surprise, but before responding, ask yourself:

» Is this better dealt with straight away or should I just acknowledge that it has been heard and deal with it later?

» Is it better dealt with in a public forum or privately?

» What is the speaker's purpose in saying this? Are they serious or is it an attempt at humour?

» Is the speaker being deliberately provocative and looking for a reaction?

Use phrases like 'I really have to challenge that statement', and 'Can we just stop and think about what you have said there'. Rather than comment on it yourself, pass it straight on to the rest of the class, saying: 'What does anybody else think about that?' This can often make learners realise what they have said without the need for you to be the arbiter.

Try to use questions rather than statements. Questions could include: 'What makes you say that?', 'Do you feel that way about every person in that group?' and 'What does anybody else think about that?' Questions provide no target to attack, whereas statements tend to make people feel defensive.

Other approaches could appeal to the speaker's view of themselves, such as 'I'm surprised to hear you say that, because I've always thought of you as a very open-minded student'. Or 'That seems a very harsh thing to say, which is not like you'. You can state how the statement makes you feel (eg 'It makes me feel uncomfortable to hear that'). Include other members of the group, asking them how they feel about the statement.

You can handle them with humour, if you think this is appropriate but challenge the assumptions and make it clear that we should not accept these stereotypes.

How to handle inappropriate comments

Table 8.1 Responding to comments

Vocational area	Context	The learner said...	How was it handled?
Construction	Eight male learners aged 25–35. Mostly apprentice site managers, on a Principles of Management Construction course.	'Well, everyone knows working on the site is real man's work. I've never seen a woman laying tarmac.'	The tutor noted the comment and asked the rest of the group what they thought about it. Some others gave examples of women working on construction on their sites and while none had seen 'a woman laying tarmac', they made the point that this did not mean they were not able to do it. One learner who had worked in the US stated that they knew of women working on laying tarmac.
Public services	16 to 24 year-olds mixed-gender class discussing attitudes towards gay and lesbian couples.	'People of my generation are pretty tolerant of gays. I know a few gays and they're all right. Older people, like you sir, are really intolerant, aren't you?'	The tutor threw the question open to the rest of the class, who reacted to her comment and stated that she was making generalisations. He also asked the learner why she thought that he was intolerant and how he (the tutor) might feel if somebody said that to him.
Business studies	Class of ten females and two males, 17 to 19 year-olds. The female tutor was moving a table.	(A female student said) 'You help her, Ant (Anthony), you're a man.'	The tutor stopped moving the table and said, 'that's interesting (student's name). Why do you think Ant should help rather than one of the girls?' Other students supported the view that girls in the group would be equally capable of moving the table and the speaker accepted it with good humour.

Table 8.1 (Cont.)

Vocational area	Context	The learner said...	How was it handled?
Elderly care	16 to 18 year-olds in a mixed-gender class discussing working in a care home.	'I'm allergic to old people. They're rude and they smell.'	The tutor asked the learner to explain more about what they meant when they said, 'allergic'. They asked the learner how they would feel if someone said these things about her grandparents.
Early years care	Mostly 16 to 18 year-old female learners discussing factors that influence a child's upbringing.	'Well, everyone knows single parents can't bring up kids properly.'	The tutor noted the comment and asked whether there was any proof behind that statement. He later asked the class to see if they could find examples of successful people who had been brought up by a single parent. (In a subsequent lesson learners came back with examples including former president Barack Obama; film stars such as Leonardo DiCaprio and Pierce Brosnan; sports stars including swimmer Michael Phelps and basketball player Lebron James; as well as musicians including Madonna and Paul McCartney.)

Look at the comments in Table 8.1, which are all real. Reflect on them and consider how you might have responded to them. If appropriate, you may use these statements with learners as starting points to discuss stereotypes and assumptions. Each statement shows what vocational area learners were working in, what was said, and how it was handled by the tutor. Ultimately, how you respond to this type of statement is up to your professional judgement and your knowledge of your learners, but what follows are some ways in which you might respond.

Remember: You don't have to change people, but you do have to raise awareness and make it clear that these are stereotypes.

The following activity has existed in various forms for many years. It can be in the guise of a hot air balloon, nuclear shelter or stranded spacecraft. This one is a lifeboat activity. The purpose of the activity is to generate debate. There is no right or wrong answer. The activity develops speaking and listening skills and forming arguments to support your view. I have adapted this version to focus on assumptions about gender, so while learning can take place in presenting and defending your case in a group discussion, the main learning point is to recognise that we make assumptions about gender stereotypes.

Activity

Teachers' notes

Read the 'Lost!' scenario below. Choose groups of between six and eight learners and allow about 30 minutes to come to a decision on which people to save. Explain that all decisions must be a consensus of the whole group and that the skills of verbal communication, team working, and persuasiveness are being looked for. At this stage do not mention anything about gender assumptions. Give one member of the group an envelope with instructions and a mark sheet containing each passenger's name and a column to tick M (Male) or F (Female). The instructions should say something like:

'Do not take part in the discussion. Listen and note down what assumptions the group make about the gender of the passengers (do they refer to them as "he" or "she"?). Mark "M" if they talk about the passenger as if they are male or "F" if they think the passenger is female. Don't let the group know what you are doing! I will tell them you are observing the discussion!'

Lost!

You are the captain of a ship. A fire onboard has destroyed the radio. From the rate the water is rising inside the ship, you estimate that it will sink in two to two-and-a-half hours. You did not tell the authorities of your destination. It will take 45 minutes to launch the boat, leaving a further 75 to 105 minutes before the ship sinks. Each person takes 15 minutes to lower into the boat; therefore, between five and seven people could be saved. They can't jump as the water is shark-infested. The nearest land is an uninhabited tropical island 30km away.

You will need to choose *five* people who will certainly be saved and a further *two* who might be saved.

Everyone has agreed to abide by the group's decision. Items held by individuals must stay with the owner; they cannot be transferred to other people.

Passenger/crew list

» **Captain:** Age 57. Married three times; five children aged between 5 and 27. Drinks and smokes heavily. Plays the accordion. Carries a bottle of rum.

» **Ship's engineer:** Married. Heroism in fighting the fire has given fellow passengers time to launch the lifeboat but has sustained severe burns. Carries a shaving mirror.

» **Radio operator:** Ex-British Navy. Brought up on a farm. A fitness fanatic and champion kickboxer. Escaped the fire which destroyed the radio. Was on deck trying to impress the food scientist with a display of kickboxing skills at the time. Carries a length of rope.

» **Cook:** A former Special Forces officer reduced to working as a cook after being court-martialled following an unfortunate incident involving a heavy night of drinking. Carries a knife.

» **Anglican priest:** A philosophy graduate who taught English as a foreign language in South America for several years before returning to home town to look after a disabled mother (now aged 85). Trained as a counsellor and was ordained in 1990. Carries a first aid kit.

» **Diving instructor:** After 20 years as a stockbroker in London, has just moved to Tahiti to set up a diving school. Divorced, with a son at boarding school in Wales. Goes grouse-shooting in Yorkshire every August. Carries a signed copy of the final Harry Potter novel.

» **Indian ship's carpenter:** Married with four children aged between six months and seven years old. Was convicted of violent affray following a demonstration in Mumbai ten years ago. Writes poetry and has had two poems published in Indian literary magazines. Has a magnifying glass.

» **French botany student:** Lived in the Brazilian rainforest for 18 months while carrying out PhD research into plants that can be used in anti-cancer drugs: these are now undergoing testing by a major multinational pharmaceutical company. Has a rifle.

» **Retired soldier:** Recently registered a civil partnership with their long-term partner, who is a 45 year-old political journalist. Together, they have campaigned for improved healthcare for soldiers wounded in Iraq. Carries a compass.

» **Food scientist:** A vegetarian whose research centres on developing plant-based, low-cholesterol alternatives to meat. Has been involved in several demonstrations against the use of animals in medical research. Carries a box of chocolate bars.

» **Nurse:** Came to Scotland eight years ago as a teenage refugee from Sudan who spoke no English on arrival. Gained six GCSEs and has recently qualified as a nurse. A devout Muslim who plans to complete the Hajj next year. Carries a box of matches.

» **Bank manager:** Lives in a village in Sussex. Guide leader, parish councillor and president of the local allotment society in spare time. Has £50,000 in used £10 notes carried in a small suitcase.

Adapted from Wake Tech's ESL Blogs Teamwork Lesson (2016)

Summary (What should I do next?)

» Decide what you understand by promoting equality and raising awareness of diversity.

» Plan how you can take opportunities to promote equality and diversity as a natural part of what you do.

» Think about how you can deal with unplanned opportunities to promote equality and diversity and raise awareness of diversity.

» Consider how you will respond to inappropriate comments.

» Think about opportunities to raise awareness of diversity in meaningful ways, for example by using the life experiences of your learners, including experience of different food, celebrations, customs and education.

Further reading

ACAS (2018) Unconscious Bias. [online] Available at: www.acas.org.uk/index.aspx?articleid=5433 (accessed 12 October 2018).

This article is a concise summary of the key points of unconscious bias and how it affects our interactions with others. It explores other aspects of bias such as the 'halo' effect (ignoring the negative and focusing only on positive aspects of a person) and affinity bias, where you may look favourably on a person because they have similar life experiences or come from the same background as you.

Equality and Human Rights Commission (2014) Equality Act 2010 – Technical Guidance on Further and Higher Education. [online] Available at: www.equalityhumanrights.com/sites/default/files/equalityact2010-technicalguidance-feandhe-2015.doc (accessed 12 October 2018).

This guidance document specifically produced for further and higher education is a useful guide to the Equality Act of 2010. Although rather wordy at over 200 pages, it contains useful advice, particularly for the definitions of the major terms used in the Act. One useful feature is case studies, which give examples of scenarios that may be encountered in further education and advise on whether they are discriminatory or not.

Project Implicit (2011) IAT Tests. [online] Available at: https://implicit.harvard.edu/implicit/takeatest.html (accessed 12 October 2018).

This site run by Harvard University allows you to take various Implicit Association Tests (IATs) to assess unconscious bias in a number of areas, including attitudes to gender, sexuality, race, and young and old people. It is well grounded in research and contains useful advice and guidelines on how to use the tests. It is a useful exercise to test your own potential bias but consider carefully if you choose to use it with learners.

Ross, H (2008) Proven Strategies for Addressing Unconscious Bias in the Workplace. *CDO Insights*, 2(5) [online] Available at: www.cookross.com/docs/UnconsciousBias.pdf (accessed 12 October 2018).

A very useful article on the power of unconscious bias on our decision making. It explores why we need unconscious bias to survive and how we can recognise and allow for it.

Online

Always #LikeAGirl (2014) Run Like a Girl. [online] Available at: www.youtube.com/watch?v=XjJQBjWYDTs (accessed 21 August 2018).

A useful three-minute video. It challenges the negative effect of the statement 'like a girl', for example 'run like a girl' and 'fight like a girl'. It is a good starting point for discussions on gender bias.

References

Citron, A F, Chein, I and Harding, J (1950) Anti-minority Remarks: A Problem for Action Research. *Journal of Abnormal and Social Psychology*, 45: 99–126.

Equality Challenge Unit (2018) Unconscious Bias. [online] Available at: www.ecu.ac.uk/guidance-resources/employment-and-careers/staff-recruitment/unconscious-bias/ (accessed 12 October 2018).

Kelly, M (2004) *The Rhythm of Life: Living Everyday with Passion and Purpose*. New York: Simon & Schuster.

Plous, S (2000) Responding to Overt Displays of Prejudice: A Role-Playing Exercise. *Teaching of Psychology*, 27(3): 198–200.

Ross, H (2008) Proven Strategies for Addressing Unconscious Bias in the Workplace. *CDO Insights*, 2(5) [online] Available at: www.cookross.com/docs/UnconsciousBias.pdf (accessed 12 October 2018).

Unionlearn, TUC (2018) Equality and Diversity – What's the Difference? [online] Available at: www.unionlearn.org.uk/equality-and-diversity-whats-difference (accessed 12 October 2018).

Wake Tech's ESL Blogs (2016) Teamwork Lesson. [online] Available at: http://eslblogs.waketech.edu/resources/wp-content/uploads/sites/23/2016/06/Level-5-Unit-8-Community-Teamwork-Lesson.pdf (accessed 12 October 2018).

Chapter 9 Promoting British values

"Values aren't buses... They're not supposed to get you anywhere. They're supposed to define who you are."

Jennifer Crusie

Introduction

Since 2015, further education and skills providers have been required to promote British values. The phrase 'fundamental British values' first appeared in the government's 2011 Prevent Strategy, published as part of its overall counter-terrorism strategy. In 2015, after allegations of extremist activity in several Birmingham schools (allegations which were never proven), the government published its 'Prevent' duty guidance, to the further education and skills sector on 18 September 2015. The Prevent duty is defined as:

"the duty in the Counter-Terrorism and Security Act 2015 on specified authorities, in the exercise of their functions, to have due regard to the need to prevent people from being drawn into terrorism."

(HM Government, 2015, p 5)

The 'Prevent' duty guidance requires staff to promote fundamental British values in the curriculum. The four fundamental British values, identified in the Prevent duty, are:

1. Democracy

Democracy involves the fundamental belief in free and fair elections to establish a government elected by the people. All people have an opportunity to elect representatives and the majority choice is respected. Discussion of the concept of democracy might arise from:

» any voting on a class issue, for example voting for class representatives or, where appropriate, voting on a choice of learning activities;

» any opportunity to observe democracy at work, for example local or general elections or news stories of elections in other countries.

2. The rule of law

Rule of law is the principle that all people, including the elected government, are subject to and accountable to the rule of law, which is applied fairly and equitably to all, regardless of their status. The guiding principle says that the law should protect individuals and ensure their safety and well-being. The rule of law might include discussion of:

» any examples of law breaking, such as events reported in daily news, breaching copyright, music or film piracy, and tax evasion.

3. Individual liberty

This is defined as the right to act, believe and express yourself in a manner of your choosing, including the right to free speech and to express your opinion without fear of intimidation or violence from others, including the government. Exceptions occur when this expression promotes violence or harm to other individuals. Discussions of the rights of the individual may include:

» the right to choose courses of action;

» freedom of speech;

» sexual preferences;

» the right to strike or protest.

4. Mutual respect and tolerance for those with different faiths and beliefs

This involves the belief that each person is an individual and should be treated with dignity and respect, together with an acceptance that people have a right to follow their own beliefs and faiths and to do so without interference. Exceptions occur when those beliefs promote violence or hatred against others. Promotion of this aspect might come from discussing:

» religious festivals such as Eid, Passover, Easter or Ramadan;

» other faiths and cultures; recognising their achievements including immigrants into Britain;

» the balance of respecting other beliefs with the requirement not to incite others to acts of terrorism;

» the nine protected characteristics as set out in the Equality Act of 2010. (It is expected that learners would have some knowledge of these characteristics.)

Think about it

Looking at the four principles of British values, think about how you might promote these values in your learning.

The Common Inspection Framework and Further Education and Skills Inspection Handbook 2018 judges the promotion of British values, under Personal Development, Behaviour and Welfare. This judgement has a clear focus on learners' preparation for their next steps in education or employment, as well as preparing them to be active citizens in society. Inspectors are asked to judge the extent to which:

> "*learning programmes, including enrichment activities, allow all learners to explore personal, social and ethical issues and take part in life in wider society and in Britain.*"
>
> **(HM Government, 2018, p 43)**

Preparing learners to '*take part in life in wider society and in Britain*' is a complex task and not one that tutors can do on their own. Good and outstanding providers will put British values at the heart of everything they do, with a whole-organisation approach to the promotion of British values.

Why 'British' values?

The introduction of fundamental British values has been not without controversy. Many teachers have questioned what is particularly 'British' about the values. Indeed, the values correlate closely to values that are widely accepted human rights. Struthers (2016, p 4) notes that '*equality, justice, non-discrimination, dignity, freedom, fairness, tolerance, respect for others and solidarity all constitute human rights values*'.

It is clear to see the similarities with the stated British values. Some organisations have renamed them 'fundamental values' or 'college values' to remove the feeling of being exclusively 'British'. In a video produced by journalist Dilly Hussain (iERA, 2015), when questioned many people either did not know what British values are or chose values which are more closely associated with personal issues such as family, friendship or compassion. It might be interesting to ask your learners what they think British values are, before introducing the government's definition.

British values in action?

It would be surprising to find anyone who would argue against the values that are identified in the policy of promoting British values. Most teachers would agree that the four key values should be promoted but may feel that the requirement to promote British values is yet another addition to the growing list of 'things' to be covered in lessons. Many view the requirements as something imposed by an external agent. To be successful in an observation you need to look at it in a different way.

Consider that the values we are talking about are values you would be promoting naturally in your teaching. For example, you are looking to be fair to every student, give them the best chance of success and not discriminate against or disadvantage them because of some characteristic. You want to ensure that all learners have an equal opportunity to contribute and all have an equal chance to produce their best. Turn taking, in group or class discussions, is democracy in action. Listening to and respecting each other's beliefs and traditions is a key part of fundamental British values. You are already promoting these values in the everyday running of your classroom. Make this explicit to learners. Relate discussions to the four key principles of British values. Look at the posters around your organisation. Ask learners about them. Do they know what they mean and how they relate to their vocational subjects and their lives in general? Look at your organisation's policy on promoting fundamental British values. Measure what it says against what you do in the classroom and see if you are meeting what it requires.

A bit of theory

The promotion of British values is closely linked to the Prevent agenda, which is the government's strategy to address the risk of terrorism. 2015/16 was the first academic year of the duty being put into practice and at the end of the year Ofsted carried out a survey entitled, *How Well are Further Education and Skills Providers Implementing the Prevent Duty?* (HM Government, 2016). The survey was carried out between November 2015 and May 2016. The evidence for the survey's findings is based on visits to 37 further education and skills providers, together with the findings of 46 full inspection reports.

What did the survey look at?

The Prevent duty guidance requires providers to have the following in place:

- » policies for the management of external speakers;
- » active engagement with partners including the police and local Prevent co-ordinators;
- » risk assessment strategies to identify where learners may be at risk of being drawn into extremist views;
- » appropriate training for all staff;
- » welfare and pastoral support including policies on the use of faith facilities such as prayer rooms;

» IT policies that specifically refer to the Prevent duty and ensure the correct use of IT equipment including social media.

The survey sought to answer the following questions about these key areas of the Prevent duty.

» Are external speakers being appropriately checked and monitored for the messages they bring?

» Are providers making the best use of partnership working with other agencies?

» Are providers assessing risks that learners may face and taking appropriate action to reduce that risk?

» How effectively do staff training and pastoral support contribute to keeping learners safe?

» Are learners being protected from inappropriate use of the internet and social media?

What did the survey find?

The survey found that general further education providers and sixth form colleges have performed better than other types of providers, but there were 'considerable variations' in the way providers have implemented the Prevent duty guidance.

Other key findings included the following.

» 22 of the 37 providers visited had implemented the Prevent duty well.

» Some providers adopted a 'tick box' approach to the implementation which goes against the government approach of adopting meaningful activities to implement the Prevent duty.

» In a third of the providers visited, at least one aspect of the Prevent agenda had not been implemented.

» Too many providers did not thoroughly check the suitability of external speakers.

» Partnership working was ineffective in several providers. Providers and local authorities failed to work well together, including local authorities focusing mainly on schools and sometimes giving conflicting advice about what providers needed to do to meet the requirements of the Prevent duty.

» In half of the providers, not enough was done to protect learners from the dangers of radicalisation through the internet and social media. In too many providers, learners were able to bypass security systems and access inappropriate materials including stories of learners accessing video of beheadings and bomb-making techniques.

» Monitoring the use of prayer rooms was a cause for concern, with too much unsupervised access and stories of groups of learners from a single faith group dominating the use of the facility.

» In a third of the providers, staff training was ineffective. Managers were trained but training for staff who have daily contact with learners was too generic. It relied too much on online training which did not take sufficient account of the specific risks in the local community.

Conclusion

While most providers have implemented the Prevent duty effectively, there is still concern that too many providers have not understood the requirements sufficiently. The survey shows that after the first year of implementation there is still work to do. Specifically, providers need to focus on:

» policies to protect learners from potential risks posed by external speakers and events;

» strong and effective partnership working including the local authority to share intelligence and access support;

» high-quality and meaningful risk assessments and action plans to protect learners from potential risks;

» effective staff development suited to the roles of the staff involved and the impact of that training measured effectively;

» ensuring that learners have a good understanding of British values and how to keep themselves safe from the threat of radicalisation. This should include clear reporting procedures and support for learners at risk;

» monitoring IT usage closely, with IT policies that make specific reference to the Prevent duty. If necessary, providers should seek support to ensure that IT systems are secure and learners are not able to access inappropriate material.

These are important messages to inform the implementation of British values and could form a checklist of how well your organisation is achieving this.

From the files

Rather than giving just one example of a lesson where the promotion of British values is either good/outstanding, or not so good, the following case studies show a range of examples from different lessons. Examples of good practice are shown in case study 1.

Case study 1

a) In an English class on the difference between fact and fiction, the tutor had displayed several types of writing and asked the learners to say whether they were fact or fiction. Examples included travel brochures, medical leaflets and instruction manuals, which the learners identified as non-fiction and poetry, and romance novels and short stories, which they identified as fiction. After the discussion one learner asked, 'Miss, is the Bible fiction or non-fiction?' The tutor replied, 'Well, that is a difficult one to answer. Some people believe that the Bible is a fictional example of stories to teach people how to behave, while others think that it a literal truth. As you know, we respect the individual's choice to believe what they wish, so for some people it is fiction and for others it is non-fiction.'

b) In a sports lesson the tutor started with an activity to identify famous sports people from basketball and football. The lesson was to be on different strategies in basketball compared to football. The five images were of: Kobe Bryant and Michael Jordan (both famous American basketball players); Gareth Southgate (the serving England football manager); Hope Powell (past manager of the England Women's football team); and Ade Adepitan (a wheelchair basketball player and television presenter who was part of Great Britain's bronze medal winning team in the 2004 Athens Olympics). Of the 18 learners present, none could recognise Hope Powell or Ade Adepitan. This led to an interesting discussion of the reasons why women and sports people with disabilities were less known than the others in the list.

c) The tutor divided the class into groups and asked them to discuss their 'rights' and put them on a flipchart. Most groups recorded rights such as the right to be respected, receive fair treatment and appreciation for people's differences. The tutor led the group feedback and recorded everyone's ideas, making sure everyone contributed and felt involved. Following that discussion, the groups were asked to look at what they felt were their 'responsibilities'. Many of the same things came up, and through a discussion learners came to realise that they needed to treat others in the way they expected to be treated themselves.

Case study 2

a) In a tutorial session learners were asked to elect a class representative. The teacher took charge of the process and wrote the names of four volunteers on the board and then asked for a show of hands so that people could vote for their preferred candidate. A large group of boys voted for their friend and he was duly elected as the class representative.

b) In a sports lesson a group of apprentice footballers were carrying out an analysis of their own football skills. A few learners engaged in the activity, some others were slow to start, and some were talking while the tutor was giving instructions.

After talking in pairs, interviewing each other using a proforma to analyse strengths and weaknesses, learners were asked to feed back their findings. Many were clearly not listening while learners were feeding back. One learner was playing with his pen, another was swinging on his chair and others were clearly losing interest. Two learners were laughing when one learner described his 'touch' as a weakness. Others chatted among themselves as the learners fed back and one learner at the back was making a great show of yawning. When another learner listed his strengths, a learner commented, 'Are you sure?' Some were sniggering when one learner was listing his weaknesses. When one learner listed his strengths as passing and reading the game, most of the class laughed.

One commented on a learner's pronunciation of 'heading' when he missed out the first 'h' and said 'edding'.

c) In one lesson there was an informal discussion of how learners travel to the provider. One learner mentioned that because he was quite small for his age, he regularly bought and travelled on a child's ticket even though he was over age.

Key learning points

The examples in case study 1 are all good examples of integrating discussion and raising awareness of British values as a natural part of the lesson. In the first example, the teacher took the opportunity to reinforce the idea of individual liberty and the right of everyone to hold their own beliefs. In the other two examples, learners were given an opportunity to discuss issues of mutual respect through the portrayal of women in sport (in the case of Hope Powell) and athletes with disabilities (in the case of Ade Adepitan). In the last example, learners improved their understanding of elements of democracy and the rule of law in discussing the rights and responsibilities of citizens and how the law supports these.

The first example in case study 2 might seem like an example of democracy, but in fact learners were not given a choice in how the class representative was elected and the voting system was not anonymous, so that some learners were intimidated into voting for one candidate. There were clearly missed opportunities to discuss the nature of a democratic voting process.

Example b may appear to have nothing to do with British values, but there is a clear lack of mutual respect and tolerance in this lesson by a significant majority of the learners, both for the teacher and for each other. There are several instances of disrespectful and intolerant behaviour. There is clearly much work to do to improve the mutual respect in that group.

Example c was an offhand remark but one that might have provided an opportunity to discuss the rule of law. The conversation would have to be handled carefully, but there is an opportunity to discuss the ethical and legal situation. For example, how did the learner feel about buying a child's ticket to travel when he was clearly over age? What, if any, are the consequences of breaking this law? Is this a victimless crime?

Think about it

Dealing with controversial issues

One of the key factors in promoting British values is how to deal with controversial issues. Many teachers lack confidence in leading discussions and addressing controversial views expressed by learners. Controversial issues are those issues which are tied into strongly held beliefs and may arouse emotional and passionate viewpoints and expressions, which may not always be open to rational consideration of evidence.

Top ten tips to handle controversial issues in discussions

1. Demonstrate that you value democracy and respect for all views. Discuss freedom of speech versus the legal requirement not to incite hatred against any group or individuals.

2. Promote an atmosphere in your sessions which values everyone's opinion and their right to express it without fear.

3. Promote an understanding that people can hold opposing views without resorting to personal attacks or insults. Help learners to appreciate that people with differing views may agree to disagree.

4. Don't be afraid to challenge personal or discriminating remarks. Make sure you challenge the remark and not the person who made it. This needs careful handling, but it is essential you separate the remark from the individual.

5. Decide when is the appropriate time to challenge or discuss controversial remarks. Some learners may adopt the tactic of using controversial remarks to distract the class or to provoke a reaction. Judge whether it is useful to discuss the issue at the time or leave it until later. However, always ensure that a challenging remark has been noted, even if you choose to deal with it later.

6. Establish clear ground rules from the start of your time with your group. Involve the group in creating these rules (use this as another example of democracy in British values). Let the group decide what should happen if people do not stick to the rules of discussion.

7. If your organisation has a policy on discussing controversial issues, make sure you know and use it. If there is no policy, consider creating one.

8. Remind learners constantly that everyone has a right to contribute, or to keep information private, if they wish. Consider having material on the walls that you can refer to, such as posters or learners' work on discussing controversial issues.

9. Build in time to reflect on learning after discussions. Consider using a reflection sheet with prompts to help learners consider their feelings and contributions to controversial discussions. These can be anonymous if you wish.

10. Model best practice in discussing controversial issues. Remain calm, even if learners become heated in their discussions. Reflect on strategies to manage discussions with different topics and groups of learners. Praise learners when they express strongly held views appropriately and listen respectfully to others' opposing opinions.

Table 9.1 Opportunities to promote British values

Vocational area	Democracy	The rule of law	Individual liberty	Mutual respect and tolerance
Business administration	• Discussion of voting systems, using examples of the results of local and general elections and their influence on business. • The politics of democracy and how which party is in power may affect business decisions.	• Following legal requirements on keeping data on customers. • Following health and safety procedures in the workplace. • Respecting working rights. • Legislation relating to companies and consumer protection.	• Achieving work–life balance. • Discussing the social effects of unemployment. • Looking at moral issues associated with business. • Discussion of ethical businesses and how individual liberties affect business decisions.	• Ensuring the office environment and customer-facing areas are accessible and welcoming to a selection of customers. • Discussion of sexism, racism and discrimination in the workplace. • Cultural differences between different customer groups and their effect on business practices.
Construction	• How rules governing the construction industry have come about. • The history of trade union pressure for safe working and improved conditions.	• Follow health and safety and working regulations and understand the need for them. • Discuss the consequences of not following building regulations. • Working safely with amenities such as gas and electricity as well as the use of PPE. • Ethics of working practices such as tax evasion by individuals and companies. • Research the Health and Safety at Work Act 1974, and other relevant legislation.	• The right to choose courses, employment and career paths to suit your needs. • The limits of individual liberty to comply with laws governing the construction industry. • Choices in terms of securing good working conditions and working hours.	• Learners' code of conduct in class. • Discussing historical practices and the reputation of building sites as portrayed in the media. • Identifying behaviours that employers expect on site and initiatives such as respectful construction sites. • Working together in multi-discipline teams respecting each other's views and opinions.

Early years care	• Encourage turn taking and sharing. • Allow children to vote for an activity by a show of hands. • Show that all questions are valued and that everyone's opinion counts.	• Knowledge of legislation relevant to childcare. • Promoting following rules with children such as playing games and rules of tidying up. • Ensuring children know right from wrong.	• Every child's views are important and we all have differences which should be respected. • Discover their own abilities, for example taking risks in physical play and discuss how they feel about it. • Allow children to learn that everyone is free to have different opinions, for example liking different foods and toys.	• Encourage playing together and supporting each other. • Finding out about and respecting beliefs and values from other traditions, for example whether children celebrate Christmas. • Provide resources that challenge stereotypes of gender, culture and race.
Motor vehicle maintenance	• How laws have come about to regulate the motor vehicle industry • Processes to make decisions in the workshop by voting on choices.	• The importance of legislation in the motor vehicle industry. • Following safe practices and adhering to health and safety laws in the workshop. • Data protection legislation in relation to the motor vehicle industry.	• The effects of environmentally friendly and sustainable production methods. • Individual choices about career paths and working conditions.	• Being aware and having respect for the needs of different client groups. • Discussing the regulations that affect how people should be treated at work, eg the Equality Act, race and sex discrimination and working time directives. • Working together as a team.

Opportunities to promote British values

Opportunities to promote British values can appear in any area. In the following table are four vocational areas and some suggestions on how British values may be promoted within each. They are not exclusive and serve as a starting point for you to think of your own examples, best suited to your context and your learners.

Summary (What should I do next?)

» Look at your lesson planning and schemes of work for opportunities to raise awareness of British values.

» Look at the four key aspects of British values (democracy; the rule of law; individual liberty; and mutual respect and tolerance) and decide how they relate to your teaching and learning and regularly make them explicit to learners.

» See the promotion of British values as something worthwhile and something you already do, rather than an extra job.

» Understand that raising awareness of British values and the skills of discussing controversial issues helps learners develop important life skills.

Further reading

Active Citizens FE (2017) British Values and Prevent Induction Activities for Post-16 Learners. [online] Available at: www.activecitizensfe.org.uk/uploads/2/2/9/1/22910514/acfe_prevent_materials_final_.3.pdf (accessed 23 July 2018).

As the title implies, these are six activities for use in induction, covering raising awareness of British values and Prevent. There are a lot of useful activities, including card-sorting activities defining terms such as 'democracy' and 'the rule of law'.

Barry, S (2017) British Values and Prevent Review 2016–17. [online] Available at: www.northkent.ac.uk/documents/2017/BritishValuesandPrevent_NKCReview_July17.docx (accessed 20 July 2018).

This contains a useful example of one college's policy on British values. It describes how the college has implemented British values and the Prevent agenda and has useful descriptions of how British values are promoted in all aspects of college life.

Pinnacle Training (2016) Promoting Fundamental British Values- Cheynes Training. [online] Available at: www.cheynestraining.com/wp-content/uploads/2017/01/Prevent-Booklet-March-2016.pdf (accessed 25 October 2018).

This useful resource produced for Cheynes Training includes definitions of terms such as 'extremism' and links to the Education and Training Foundation (ETF) website containing advice on implementing the Prevent strategy in FE. There are resources for use in staff development and activities to use with learners, including useful links to video clips, such as 'What is a democracy?'

Tyreman, H (2017) Teaching Practice – British Values. [online] Available at: https://hannahruthtyreman.wordpress.com/2017/02/27/british-values/ (accessed 12 October 2018).

This is a very useful article containing a range of advice on British values from a teacher in South Yorkshire. There are useful tips on preparing for Ofsted inspection, as well as several activities to use with staff and learners. There is a particularly useful section with examples of how to challenge learners' views.

References

Crusie, J (Goodreads) (2013) Jennifer Crusie Quotes. [online] Available at: www.goodreads.com/author/quotes/19005.Jennifer_Crusie (accessed 12 October 2018).

HM Government (2011) *Prevent* Strategy. [online] Available at: https://assets.publishing.service.gov.uk/government/uploads/system/uploads/attachment_data/file/97976/prevent-strategy-review.pdf (accessed 23 July 2018).

HM Government (2015) *Prevent* Duty Guidance for Further Education Institutions in England and Wales. [online] Available at: www.legislation.gov.uk/ukdsi/2015/9780111133309/pdfs/ukdsiod_9780111133309_en.pdf (accessed 12 October 2018).

HM Government (2016) How Well are Further Education and Skills Providers Implementing the Prevent Duty? [online] Available at: https://assets.publishing.service.gov.uk/government/uploads/system/uploads/attachment_data/file/543937/How_well_are_further_education_and_skills_providers_implementing_the__Prevent__duty.pdf (accessed 12 October 2018).

HM Government (2018) Further Education and Skills Inspection Handbook 2018. [online] Available at: https://assets.publishing.service.gov.uk/government/uploads/system/uploads/attachment_data/file/696842/Further_education_and_skills_inspection_handbook_April_2018.doc.pdf (accessed 23 July 2018).

iERA (2015) What are British Values? [online] Available at: www.youtube.com/watch?v=Up tHOWrcd9A&feature=youtu.be (accessed 12 October 2018).

Struthers, A (2016) Teaching British Values in Our Schools but Why Not Human Rights Values? [online] Available at: http://journals.sagepub.com/doi/10.1177/09646639 16656752 (accessed 19 July 2018).

Appendix 1

Teacher reflective journal

Date/Time/ Group	Event	Experience	Reflection	Learning
Details of date, time and group taught.	What did I try?	What happened?	Why did it happen?	What did I learn? What could I do next time?

Appendix 2

Find the words starter activity

This was recommended in Chapter 2 as a starter activity.

Below are 300 words that can be made from the letters of the word 'confidentiality'.

You might not want to use all 300, but you can pick out sets of words to give to learners after the exercise, to reinforce some learning points such as:

» building spellings from root words, eg 'diet' to 'dietician' or 'confidential' to 'confidentiality';

» looking at double letters in spellings such as 'flat' and 'flatten' and 'fat' and 'fatten';

» asking learners what happens to the first vowel sound in each of the following words: 'din' and 'dine'; 'dot' and 'dote'; 'not' and 'note'; 'cod' and 'code'; and 'con' and 'cone'. Is there a pattern that might help them in their spelling?

» selecting words to extend learners' vocabulary in their chosen vocational area. For example, explore the meaning and discuss in which vocational contexts learners might use the following words (some suggestions are given in brackets):

  – 'acid', 'acidity', 'dietician' and 'dialect' (health care, childcare);

  – 'antidote', 'clot', 'canine' and 'fatten' (veterinary, animal care), 'clone' and 'cloned' in these areas provides an opportunity to discuss ethical issues if appropriate;

  – 'cadet', 'cite', 'citation', 'incite' and 'yield' (public services);

» choosing to work on homophones such as 'ail' and 'ale'; 'faint' and 'feint'; 'tale' and 'tail'; 'lane' and 'lain'.

300 words from the word 'confidentiality'

1.	ace	11.	alien	21.	ate
2.	acid	12.	aloft	22.	atone
3.	acidity	13.	alone	23.	atoned
4.	act	14.	and	24.	attend
5.	acted	15.	annoy	25.	cadet
6.	action	16.	annoyed	26.	cafe
7.	actioned	17.	ant	27.	calf
8.	aid	18.	antidote	28.	can
9.	ail	19.	any	29.	candle
10.	ale	20.	anyone	30.	candy

31. cane	64. cold	97. dental
32. caned	65. colt	98. deny
33. canine	66. con	99. detail
34. canny	67. cone	100. detain
35. cannot	68. confide	101. dial
36. canoe	69. confident	102. dialect
37. canon	70. confine	103. dice
38. cent	71. confined	104. dictate
39. citadel	72. contain	105. dictation
40. citation	73. contained	106. die
41. cite	74. content	107. diet
42. cited	75. cot	108. dietician
43. city	76. coy	109. din
44. clad	77. day	110. dine
45. clan	78. daily	111. ditty
46. clay	79. dainty	112. ditto
47. clean	80. dale	113. doe
48. clod	81. dance	114. dole
49. clone	82. dane	115. donate
50. cloned	83. date	116. done
51. clot	84. deaf	117. dot
52. clotted	85. deal	118. dote
53. cloy	86. dealt	119. dye
54. cloyed	87. dean	120. eat
55. coal	88. defiant	121. élan
56. coat	89. defiantly	122. elf
57. cod	90. deft	123. end
58. code	91. deftly	124. enfold
59. codify	92. defy	125. entail
60. coil	93. delay	126. entity
61. coiled	94. den	127. face
62. coin	95. denial	128. faced
63. coined	96. dent	129. facile

130. facility
131. fact
132. fad
133. fade
134. fail
135. failed
136. faint
137. fainted
138. fan
139. fancied
140. fancy
141. fat
142. fate
143. fated
144. fatted
145. fatten
146. field
147. feint
148. fen
149. fend
150. fiend
151. fidelity
152. fin
153. final
154. finale
155. finance
156. fine
157. fined
158. find
159. finite
160. file
161. filed
162. fit

163. fitted
164. flan
165. flat
166. flatten
167. fled
168. float
169. floated
170. foal
171. foil
172. foiled
173. fold
174. fond
175. fondly
176. font
177. idea
178. ideal
179. idiocy
180. idiot
181. idiotic
182. idle
183. idol
184. in
185. incident
186. incidental
187. incite
188. infancy
189. infant
190. infanticide
191. infantile
192. infidel
193. innate
194. intact
195. intend

196. intent
197. iota
198. italic
199. lad
200. laden
201. lady
202. lain
203. land
204. lane
205. late
206. latte
207. lead
208. leaf
209. leafy
210. lean
211. led
212. left
213. lend
214. lent
215. let
216. lice
217. lido
218. lie
219. lied
220. life
221. line
222. lined
223. linnet
224. lint
225. lion
226. lit
227. load
228. loan

229. lode
230. loft
231. lofty
232. lot
233. nail
234. nailed
235. nation
236. neat
237. neatly
238. nice
239. nicely
240. nicety
241. nine
242. none
243. not
244. notated
245. note
246. noted
247. notice
248. noticed
249. oat
250. ode
251. of
252. often

253. oil
254. oily
255. oiled
256. once
257. one
258. only
259. tacit
260. tact
261. tacitly
262. tactile
263. tail
264. tailed
265. taint
266. tainted
267. tale
268. talent
269. talon
270. tan
271. tannoy
272. tea
273. ten
274. tend
275. tent
276. tidal

277. tide
278. tidy
279. tile
280. tiled
281. tilt
282. tilted
283. tin
284. tint
285. tiny
286. titan
287. titanic
288. toad
289. today
290. toil
291. ton
292. tonal
293. tone
294. toned
295. total
296. tote
297. toy
298. yet
299. yield
300. yodel

Appendix 3

Commentary on case study 1, Chapter 3

After reading case study 1 in Chapter 3, compare your findings with the commentary below.

1. What comments would you make about the stated learning outcomes?

The learning outcomes are useful as far as they go. It would be interesting to see how these outcomes will be judged. For example, how will the tutor know if all learners can tell the difference between a formal and informal letter (or email, or article on a topic)? What about expressing the learning outcome as a target, for example judging whether learners can successfully identify three examples of formal writing and three examples of informal writing?

Similarly, how will you know if all learners can plan and/or write a letter of complaint? It would be useful to have some success criteria that learners can use to gauge how well they have been able to produce an effective letter of complaint. You could use exam board criteria to familiarise learners with the expected outcomes. These criteria could be included in the learning outcomes sheet that learners might refer to throughout the lesson.

2. What use could be made of the information provided in the session file? What other information would be useful to have on each learner?

Information on previous grades at GCSE and the results of initial assessment are a useful starting point and is something that is often included in profiles, but if that information is going to result in effective differentiation for learners I would suggest that we need to go further than that. Knowing that a learner missed out on a Grade C/Level 4 in maths by one mark can be useful background information but of more use is what we do with that information. Identifying each learner's particular strengths and areas for improvement in their subject area and in their levels of English and maths is the ideal, but in practice may be very difficult to achieve if you have large numbers of students. Focusing on one area of improvement and following it through so that the learner makes good progress and 'masters' that one skill would be good.

As well as learners' past achievement (or non-achievement) and their present progress, the particular needs and attitudes towards learning can be useful background information and serve to remind tutors of the individual nature of each student. Additionally, it can be very useful for anyone observing the learning to have background information on each learner. This usually takes the form of a class profile and can be invaluable in any post-observation discussion of the effectiveness of the learning for each individual.

3. Could the task of composing a complaint be related to the different vocational areas?

In this session all learners were given the same scenario (posting a response to a poor review on a holiday review site). It might have been better to adjust the task slightly to relate to the vocational areas represented in the group, so that the response was to a bad review for a meal (catering); a faulty product (customer service); or a poor experience at the salon (hairdressing).

4. How effective is the learning in the activity of bringing learners to the front to discuss the information they would include in the complaint?

Inviting learners to the front of the class to speak is a common activity. Often it is conducted in the way described here. Learners come to the front individually or in small groups and make their presentations. This in itself can be a major achievement for many learners. In this example, learners are thanked, receive a round of applause and retreat to the safety of the crowd. I feel there is a valuable opportunity missed to help learners develop skills and confidence in speaking in front of others. Comments and suggestions on posture, clarity of voice, eye contact with the audience and even what to do with your hands would be useful skills to develop in this situation. If you know your learners well, you can carry this out with sensitivity, help develop these skills for each learner and demonstrate real differentiation.

5. What comments would you make about the final assessment activity?

This kind of self-assessment is a good idea and should not always be left to the end of the session. In this session learners completed the task individually. It might be that the tutor will take the self-assessments and use the information to build into the learning for the next session. Let's hope so. At the least the tutor should share this intention with learners and let them know what use will be made of the information they are supplying. The tutor could have gained more from the activity (and provided themselves with less work) by asking learners to compare self-assessments and pick out, say, one target for the next lesson. In this way the tutor will have clear, individual, differentiated targets for each learner.

Index